WITHDRAWN

Why Information Systems Fail

HENRY C. LUCAS, JR.

Why
Information Systems
Fail

COLUMBIA UNIVERSITY PRESS

NEW YORK AND LONDON

1975

Henry C. Lucas, Jr. is an associate professor in the
Graduate School of Business Administration,
New York University.

Library of Congress Cataloging in Publication Data

Lucas, Henry C
  Why information systems fail.

  Bibliography: p.
  1. Management information systems. I. Title.
T58.6.L83   658.4'03   74-18395
ISBN 0-231-03792-9

to
M.D.K.
and
A.G.K.

preface

DURING THE PAST DECADE, organizations have developed large numbers of computer-based information systems. Unfortunately, many of these systems must be classified as failures. Some systems have been withdrawn because they have proved unworkable, and others continue to operate though no one uses their output.

The design and operation of information systems have long been considered primarily technical activities. While there are still technical problems to be solved, we have adequate technology today to develop sophisticated information systems. Because of our concern over technology we seem to have ignored the fact that almost all information systems exist within the context of an organization. If we adopt an organizational perspective, a large number of variables must be added to existing models of the development and the operation of computer-based information systems.

The purpose of this book is to present a descriptive model of information systems in the context of the organization and to test the model with empirical data from six studies. These studies, conducted by the author, involve over 2000 users in 16 organizations. The model and studies are focused on crucial organizational behavior variables in information systems activities because they have received so little attention in the literature. There is a large body of knowledge on technical problems with information systems; these issues are not discussed at length here.

The book is intended for researchers, students, and practicing managers in user departments or the information services department. It could be used as a text or as supplemental reading in a course on systems design or information systems; it would be particularly salient in a course on the management of information systems.

For the researcher or student who is interested in the methodology and results, data are presented in detail. The more casual reader will probably want to read the introductory material in Chapters 1 and 2 and the implications in the last chapter. This reader may also want to examine the summary tables at the end of Chapters 4 through 6 to see the extent to which each proposition from the model is supported.

A number of individuals have contributed to the studies presented here. The support of Keane Associates of Wellesley, Massachusetts, and the Data Processing Management association were very helpful in the Six-Company study described in Chapter 3. The research in the Branch Bank study and Laboratory Experiment was sponsored in part by National Science Foundation Grant CJ-41257.

Messrs. Rodney Plimpton and Jimmy Sutton made a significant contribution to data collection and analysis in the San Francisco Bay Area study. Mr. Kenneth Clowes processed many of the data for the Sales Force and Branch Bank studies; he was assisted in the latter study by Mr. Pierre Romelaer. Finally, Mr. Robert Gilbertson participated in the research design, reprogrammed the Transportation Management game for the experiment, conducted the playing sessions, and prepared many of the data. Dr. Norman Nielsen also contributed to the experiments and commented on earlier versions of the manuscript.

Messrs. Kenneth Clowes, Dennis Colemen, Robert Gilbertson, Robert Kaplan, Jean Claude Larreche, and Jimmy Sutton reviewed earlier versions and offered many worthwhile suggestions. My wife Ellen has again proved to be invaluable in the preparation of the text. She managed to provide a home environment conducive to writing and made a significant contribution in reviewing the drafts of the manuscript. Simultaneously, she has managed to take care of the author and Scott, who, in his second year of life, is far more interested in the things that can be done with a piece of paper than in the words it may contain!

June 1974   HENRY C. LUCAS, JR.

contents

Why Information Systems Fail

CHAPTER
ONE

introduction

THE INFORMATION SYSTEMS FIELD

IN THE LAST TWO DECADES a new and dynamic activity has developed within organizations: the design and operation of computer-based information systems. The information services department, a new organizational subunit, has been created and made responsible for the design and operation of information systems for the organization. The nature of information systems activities and the large number of individuals involved in them create challenging problems for management and the organization.

In the last ten years the field of information systems has also begun to develop academically; business schools in particular are creating information system courses and programs (Ashenhurst, 1972). The development of an academic field has resulted in research on some of the important problems in information systems design and operation. The purpose of this book is to present a descriptive model and research results which should help to improve the probability of developing and operating successful information systems in organizations.

Information systems exist to support decisionmaking (Lucas, 1973a). Information itself is some tangible or intangible entity which reduces uncertainty about a future state or event. For example, a weather forecast for ''clear and sunny'' reduces our uncertainty about whether a baseball game scheduled for tomorrow will be played. Information systems existed long before computers were invented. However, the advent of high speed electronic computers has made the manipulation of large amounts of data fast and relatively inexpensive. Because of the computational abilities and speed of computer systems the development of more sophisticated and larger scale information systems within organizations is possible. We are primarily concerned with computer-based information systems here, though much of the discussion is pertinent to all types of information systems.

Information systems have the potential for drastically improving management and decisionmaking in an organization. Unfortunately, the success of information systems has been too narrowly defined in the past; only technical criteria have been considered. The success of an information system is highly dependent upon the relationship between users and the information services department and on the use of the system. Concentration on the technical aspects of systems and a tendency to overlook organizational behavior problems and users are the reasons most information systems have failed.

Problem Areas

We have conducted research in a number of organizations which are described in more detail in subsequent chapters. One of the data collection techniques employed was the administration of questionnaires to users of information systems in these organizations. Each of the questionnaires asked for general comments at the end of the structured questions. An analysis of the user comments indicates that there are crucial problems of an organizational behavior nature in the design and operation of information systems. All the difficulties discussed below have been mentioned at least once on questionnaires and in interviews, and most of the problems have been mentioned repeatedly. In the following discussion we do not want to suggest that every organization has experienced these problems with all of its systems. However, these problems have occurred before and the potential exists for them to continue to occur.

According to this research, users do not understand much of the output they receive; there is duplication of input and output, and changes are frequently made in systems without consulting users. Because of inaccuracies, users often discount all of the information provided by a system. Many users complain of information overload; massive amounts of data are provided which cannot be digested by the decisionmaker. There are also many complaints about the difficulty of obtaining changes in existing systems. A number of users report that they do not actually use the information provided by an information system. Many feel that computer-based information systems are not worth the time or cost to develop and that the organization would be better off without them.

To us it appears that many of these information systems would have to be classified as failures. [If a system is not used, it cannot be considered a success even if it functions well technically.] Most of the problems described above are organizational behavior problems in nature. Of course, we recognize that systems can fail for technical reasons related to hardware and software; however, technical problems with information systems are much better understood today than are organizational behavior difficulties. Though we have collected a large amount of data through interviews and questionnaires, in view of all the information systems in existence we have still only sampled a small number of organizations and information systems. However, all our experience suggests that the primary cause for system failure has been organizational behavior problems. We invite the reader to consider his own experience with information systems and judge for himself whether it is consistent with our conclusions.

In the remainder of this section we discuss some of the problems in the design and operation of information systems. Our analysis focuses on organizational behavioral considerations which have often been ignored by the information services department and users.

Systems Design

One of the major activities of the information services department is the design of new information systems, which is a time-consuming and labor-intensive process. A design team is usually formed, and it consists of personnel from the information services department and from user groups. Design is a creative task involving behavioral and technical challenges. User needs must be understood and the specifications for a system developed. These specifications have to be translated into computer processing requirements which can be executed routinely after the system becomes operational. Finally, the new system has to be validated and implemented.

One major design problem which has been consistently overlooked is how information is used by a decisionmaker. Systems have been designed to provide data without considering the types of use of the information. As we shall see later in this chapter, many information systems have been developed for fairly simple decisions or merely to process transactions; the lack of understanding of the use of information in these instances results in user annoyance and inconvenience because the wrong data or excessive amounts of data are provided. As more sophisticated systems are designed, understanding the use of information will become more critical.

In addition to understanding user needs and the use of information, there are three major problem areas in systems design and implementation. The first is technical and includes designing a system, writing programs, testing the systems, and converting the old files and procedures to the new system. Another problem category is organizational: new work relationships are established; changes are made in job content; and the structure of the organization may be affected by a system. Organizational problems include user cooperation in design, resistance to change, and modifications in the distribution of power among organizational subunits.

The final systems-design problem area is project management. Management must coordinate users, the computer staff, and possibly consultants and must manage the development of a system. Specifications must be developed and met on time and within the original cost estimates. This management task has proved to be very difficult and the attainment of original goals elusive. The major attention in improving information systems until the present has been on technical problems. However, recently interest has been stimulated in some of the managerial difficulties of developing systems (Kay, 1969; Jones and McLean, 1970).

It should be clear from this brief discussion that it is virtually impossible to develop an information system in isolation; many groups in the organization are involved. Even for systems supporting a single decision-maker, computer personnel from a subunit other than the user's must work with him. Thus new interpersonal relationships are established as information systems are developed. For some of the new applications a number of functional areas in the organization will use a single system, requiring more coordination among these areas. Such systems introduce new dependencies among the subunits and between the information services department and the subunits. A major new department which is responsible for information systems has developed, and the increasing power of this new subunit has an impact on the structure of the organization. New dependencies and power relationships among departments as a result of the development of an information system can create major organizational behavior problems

Operations

Once a system has been implemented, it is usually operated on a routine basis by the information services department. The ongoing relationship between users and the operations staff is a crucial determinant of the success of the system. The activities associated with the operation of systems are more routine than those involved in systems design, but they are equally important.

For a batch computer system the operations staff must collect input and process it. Most systems include some type of input editing; errors must be corrected before the current run or by the next processing cycle. The output from processing must be checked to be certain that the system performed properly (no program, including "operational" systems, is ever fully debugged. The output must be distributed to users, some of whom probably had little to do with supplying the input. A major problem for the operations staff is scheduling all of the production; the situation is similar to the job shop scheduling problem in operations research literature. There are a number of different jobs with different priority levels and completion schedules. Also, the operations staff is usually responsible for fixing production programs when errors are found.

For an on-line system the operations staff does not provide the bulk of input and output; users of the system are responsible instead. However, the system must be kept operational; users become dependent on on-line systems and "downtime" is very aggravating. Often an on-line system operates on the same computer system with batch processing, and thus another dimension is added to the problems of managing and scheduling operations.

On the surface it appears that the major problems in the operation of systems are related to routine scheduling and production decisions; however, there are also important behavioral considerations. To meet processing schedules, cooperation is required from users. It is easy for errors in data to create problems for the operations staff. If users are dissatisfied with the system or its operation, they can easily sabotage the information services department by withholding input, making intentional errors, etc. The information services department can also create problems for users by running jobs late or making unreasonable demands for input. The operation of systems tends to reduce the user's power and control over the process and increase the power of the information services unit.

Systems design and operations have been described as separate activities, but they are interrelated. It may be impossible to operate a system which has been badly designed. On the other hand, a successfully designed system may fail if it is impossible to operate within the time requirements established by the designers. Often organizations develop new systems without considering the burden placed on operations or the processing requirements of the system. Because month end and year end processing usually presents severe peaking problems, new systems designed to be run at this time need to be coordinated with the operations staff. Systems designers are also dependent upon the operations staff for test time to debug programs on a day-to-day basis.

Implications

An information system exists within the context of the organization; the problems of information systems are not solely technical in nature. Though there are technical problems and challenges, we have always been more successful in solving these problems than in dealing with organizational issues. It is our contention that *the major reason most information systems have failed is that we have ignored organizational behavior problems in the design and operation of computer-based information systems*. If steps are not taken to understand and solve these organizational behavior problems, systems will continue to fail.

PURPOSE

Focus of Research

This book presents a descriptive model of the organizational behavior-variables associated with the design, operation, and use of information systems in organizations. The goal of the model is to help us understand why information systems have failed and to suggest actions to prevent their continued failure. Empirical studies are discussed which provide evidence to support the model. Much of the research reported here is exploratory; however, because of the crucial nature of these behavioral problems, we hope that this effort will stimulate and guide further research.

Preview

In the remainder of this chapter we present a framework for decisionmaking and communicating about information systems. The results of several surveys of existing information systems are discussed to present a picture of the capabilities of present systems and to explore future trends in systems development. In Chapter 2 we present a descriptive model of information systems within the context of the organization. Chapter 3 contains a description of the six empirical studies which provide data relating to the descriptive model. In Chapter 4 the empirical results from studies relating to the portion of the model concerned with user attitudes and perceptions are presented. Chapters 5 and 6 present the empirical results of studies on the use of information and individual and organizational performance. In Chapter 7 we summarize the research findings and the descriptive model and discuss their implications for management, users, and the information services department.

A FRAMEWORK FOR INFORMATION SYSTEMS

Decisionmaking

The focus of our definition of information systems is on decisionmaking. Simon has described three major components of the decisionmaking process (Simon, 1965). The first is Intelligence, which involves searching the environment or becoming aware of the situation that requires a decision. During the Design stage the decisionmaker must enumerate and evaluate the alternatives available. In the Choice phase the decisionmaker selects from the alternative delineated during Design. It is also useful to add another step to Simon's model: Implementation, the process of carrying out the decision.

Information systems have the potential for supporting all parts of the decisionmaking process outlined above. During the Intelligence phase, exception reports alert the decisionmaker to a problem. (This activity corresponds to problem finding as described by Pounds, 1969.) For example, an information system may forecast liquidity for meeting cash requirements. During the Design phase the information system may present different alternatives, such as a list of sources of capital, interest rates, available lines of credit, and past borrowing history. The system may aid in the evaluation of alternatives by providing calculations which show the lowest cost options under several alternatives.

For the Choice stage it may be possible for the decisionmaker to specify a decision rule which can be executed automatically by a computer system. One rule might be to use a certain proportion of funds from each line of credit. During Implementation of the decision an information system may monitor progress to see that the decision rules have been followed. For example, has there been a sufficient inflow of funds, given the additional credit? The system can continue checking and projecting requirements for cash.

An Information Systems Framework

For discussion purposes it is helpful to have a common framework for viewing information systems; one of the clearest and most useful is Robert Anthony's framework for planning and control (Anthony, 1965). This particular framework focuses on decisions and is particularly appropriate since information systems exist to support decisionmaking. The framework is also useful because it distinguishes the different information requirements associated with different categories of decisions.

Anthony's first decision category is strategic planning, which is "the process of deciding on objectives of the organization, on changes in these objectives, on the resources used to obtain these objectives, and on the policies that are used to govern the acquisition use and disposition of these resources" (Anthony, 1965, p. 24). Strategic planning is associated with long range decisions made on an infrequent basis. Managerial control decisions, on the other hand, deal primarily with personnel and financial issues. Managerial control is defined as "the process by which managers assure that resources are obtained and used effectively and efficiently in the accomplishment of the organization's objectives" (Anthony, 1965, p. 27). The last decision category is operational control, which is "the process of assuring specific tasks are carried out effectively and efficiently" (Anthony, 1965, p. 69). Operational control as contrasted with strategic planning is concerned with the day-to-day operations of the firm. The type of information associated with each decision category is shown in Table 1.1.

While the categories have been presented as discrete, they really form a continuum. It is not possible to classify a decision exclusively in one certain category. However, the framework is useful in providing a general descriptive model of decisions and the nature of the information associated with each decision type.

Table 1.1. Information Requirements for Decision Types

Characteristic of Information	Operational Control	Management Control	Strategic Planning
Decisionmaker	Foremen, clerks	—	Top management
Source	Largely internal	—	Largely external
Complexity	Simple	—	Complex
Level of aggregation	Detailed	—	Aggregated, summary
Frequency of reporting	Frequent	—	Infrequent

Technology

One use for the framework is to identify the common fallacy of equating the sophistication of computer equipment with the sophistication of the decision or information system. A technologically complex computer system does not necessarily mean that a complex decision is supported. Technically sophisticated on-line systems are frequently dedicated to operational control applications or transactions processing. For example, an airline reservation system is very sophisticated in terms of the computer equipment and telecommunications involved; however, the data are of a transaction of operation control nature. Such a system is vitally important to the success of the organization, but it is primarily related to the day-to-day operations of the firm.

An examination of the nature of the information required for strategic planning (that is, aggregate data, limited accuracy, infrequent updating, etc.) suggests that such systems rarely require an on-line, sophisticated computer system for maintaining data. Passenger load factors which might be useful in long range planning can easily be produced as a batch processing report on a monthly basis from the data collected by an airline reservations system. A decisionmaker may desire on-line access for data manipulation and analysis; however, this can be provided through a simple time-sharing system. For example, the decisionmaker may want to examine seasonality trends or perform statistical analyses of the load characteristics for different flights. Technology and the complexity of the decision supported by an information system are not necessarily correlated. In fact, the complexity of the decision and the technology of the underlying computer system may be inversely related! In the remainder of the book the terms ''complex'' and ''sophisticated'' information systems refer to the underlying decisions involved, not the technology.

EXISTING INFORMATION SYSTEMS

On the basis of the framework, what types of information systems have been developed to date? As one might expect, the first applications areas arose in the operational control area. These systems show more tangible savings, such as inventory or personnel reductions. They tend to be associated with the automation of repetitive information flows and paperwork rather than decisionmaking. Several empirical studies provide evidence of the status of most information systems in the United States today.

The first study by Churchill was conducted in a number of organizations through interviews with managers, users, and computer department management (Churchill *et al.,* 1969). The general conclusions from this study were that the literature presents a far more advanced picture of computer usage than actually exists. Computers have achieved a great deal in clerical applications; however, their impact on management has been rather small. There is a trend toward delegating decisions to computers. New applications tend to be broad in scope; it appears that computers are being used as more than bookkeeping tools. New systems are being designed which cross a number of functional areas and subunits within the organization. Unfortunately, management of the computer resource is characterized by isolation; generally it is left to the non-management, technically oriented staff.

In another study by Brady, interviews with 100 top managers failed to locate a single individual who employed computer outputs or made direct enquiries of a computer system for decisionmaking (Brady, 1967). Few top managers received any type of information directly from a computer-based information system. Where such information did reach a top manager, the computer-based data were provided as supporting evidence for recommendations from a lower level of management. Brady concluded that the only effect computer-based information systems were having on top management was through reports prepared by middle managers using output generated by a computer-based information system.

The lack of a major impact of computer-based systems on management was also found in a study by Whisler and Meyer (1967). This research project was concerned with firms in the life insurance industry; a questionnaire was completed by a representative in each firm. The findings showed that most of the computer systems in the life insurance companies were used for clerical work. There were too few responses relating to the impact of computers on managerial jobs for a quantitative analysis. However, the impression of the authors was that computer-based information systems required increased managerial skills.

The results of these studies are consistent with the findings of a San Francisco Bay Area survey conducted by the author (Lucas, 1974a). In this study, 20 representative systems from several applications areas were studied. These systems were major ones; trivial runs or utility programs were not included. The basic unit of analysis was the report. The lead systems analyst was interviewed for each application to determine where reports were sent and what was the nature of their intended use, and the data were coded by the researchers. (Naturally, the analyst's perception of intended use may be quite different from that of the recipient of the report; an interesting follow-up study would be to compare the reaction of the user with the forecast of the analyst.)

The number of reports was used as a surrogate measure for the number of decisions supported. For batch processing systems this is not an unreasonable assumption, since reports are designed for a single decision-maker. For on-line systems such a surrogate measure would be highly suspect, but in the sample there were only two such systems—less than 1% of the total reports. In fact, of the 628 reports coded in the study, only 150 went to more than one decisionmaker and 35 to more than two decisionmakers who had the potential for using the report for another decision.

Table 1.2 shows the types of systems found in the study. First it was

Table 1.2. A Study of Bay Area Information Systems

Variable	*Categories*	*Results* % Reports in Each Category
Decision type	None	11
	Execution of rule	64
	Operational control	14
	Managerial control/strategic planning	10
Purpose of Report (complexity of problem)	Product	8
	Historical	31
	Maintenance of system	23
	Problem/action	12
	Cost	22
	Planning/trend	5
Decisionmaker	None/outside company	4
	Clerk	27
	"Super" clerk [a]	19
	Foreman/supervisor	16
	Accountant	24
	Middle/top management	11
Report frequency	Daily	16
	Weekly/semiweekly	33
	Monthly/semimonthly	33
	Other (quarterly, yearly, on request)	18
Aggregation (format)	Full report	64
	Exception report	16
	Summary report	20

[a] For example, a production control scheduler.

necessary to add two new decision categories to Anthony's framework: "None" and "Execution of a rule." For these categories no decision or a very trivial one was involved; the decision could not even be classified as operational control. They might be described as "transactions processing," and they fall below the operational control category of the Anthony continuum. Most of the reports used were historical or were for systems maintenance purposes. The decisionmaker involved was generally a clerk, foreman, or accountant; only 11% of the reports affected management. There were some summary and exception reports, though most exception reports were used by the computer department for error control.

All of these empirical studies support the observation that computer systems have had a small impact on the decisions made by most members of the organizations, especially management. Most present applications have not been complex in terms of decisionmaking. These transactions-oriented and operational control systems should be the easiest to implement, yet accounts of unsuccessful systems and negative user reactions indicate that many such systems have failed. If we have not succeeded in designing and operating relative unsophisticated information systems, how can we succeed as more complex decision processes are supported? In the remainder of the book we examine a descriptive model and research results which should improve the probability of successfully designing and operating information systems in organizations.

CHAPTER

TWO

a descriptive model

IN THIS CHAPTER we present a descriptive model of information systems in the context of the organization which focuses on organizational behavior variables. The fact that many of these variables have been ignored in the design and operation of information systems is the reason so many systems have failed. Hopefully, the results of testing the model with empirical data will make it possible to use the descriptive model for the purpose of predicting the impact of information systems on users and the organization. Such a predictive model would suggest ways to solve organizational behavior problems in the design and operation of information systems in general. A valid model would also be helpful to a specific organization in planning and managing information systems activities.

TWO ORGANIZATIONAL MODELS

Two organizational behavior models provide background on the relationship between information systems and the organization. These models of power and conflict provide perspective and suggest reasons why organizational behavior problems need to be considered in the development and operation of information systems. The models clearly demonstrate that information systems do not exist in isolation; they have the potential for creating major changes in power relationships and stimulating conflict in the organization (Lucas, 1973b).

A Power Model

Recently a theory of organizational power has been developed which focuses on subunits of the organization as the unit of analysis rather than on individuals (Hickson *et al.*, 1971). The model relates the amount of power held by a subunit to four variables: uncertainty, substitutability, work flow centrality and immediacy, and the control of strategic contingencies. According to the model, the more a subunit copes with uncertainty, the more power it will have. For routine information systems the user depends on the operations group of the information services department to produce output accurately and on schedule. The output of the information services department controls some of the uncertainty the user experiences in his work. The department also produces information which can be used to reduce a decisionmaker's uncertainty. During systems design, the information services department designs a new system which assumes some of the functions the user controlled in the past. Here the information services department has created uncertainty for the user which only the information services department can resolve.

The power model also indicates that, the greater the indispensability of a subunit, the greater is its power. There are few alternatives to the information services department, particularly if the department already exists and the organization has its own computer equipment.

The power model further hypothesizes that, the greater the pervasiveness and the immediacy of work flows, the greater is the power of a subunit. If work flows are highly interdependent among subunits, then a key department will be powerful. Immediacy of work flows refers to the speed with which a problem in one department affects others. Depending on the nature of the application, the information services department may have high work flow pervasiveness and immediacy. For example, interruption of on-line service in a reservation system can drastically affect the functioning of other departments in the organization.

The final variable in the power model is the control of contingencies; the more control of other subunits' strategic contingencies by a subunit, the greater is its power. Control over strategic contingencies relates to the interdependence between subunits; if A controls many of B's contingencies, then B is dependent upon A. One of the unique aspects of the information services department is its relationship with a number of different areas and subunits within the organization. For both the operation and the design of information systems, the information services department controls many contingencies for other subunits.

The information services department has a high score on all the variables in the power model, though the concentration of power in this subunit is often unrecognized. When information systems are implemented, there has been a tendency to focus on each individual application and not see the entire impact of all systems on the organization. The information services staff and users have ignored the gradual transfer of power to the information services department and the problems this may create. Users have become more powerless and more frustrated without understanding the reasons or even recognizing that the problem exists. The frustration and uneasiness are reflected in unfavorable attitudes toward information systems and the information services staff. Unfavorable attitudes influence user cooperation with and use of information systems.

A Conflict Model

A model has been proposed which enumerates a number of conditions leading to conflict in the organization (Walton and Dutton, 1969). The information services department has the potential for achieving a high score on all these conditions, though the following discussion is not intended to imply that any one information services department meets all of the conflict conditions. The conditions for conflict include:

Mutual task dependence
Asymmetrical work relationships
Different performance criteria and rewards
Differentiation
Role dissatisfaction
Ambiguities
Dependence on common resources
Personal skills and traits
Communications obstacles

The information services department increasingly controls strategic contingencies for other departments, as discussed for the power model; other departments depend on the information services department. That department also depends on the users for input, error correction, and assistance in designing systems. The interdependence between user depart-ments and the information services department forms a link between the power and conflict models.

The relationship between users and the information services department is asymmetric because the information services staff often feels it must understand users' jobs, whereas the reverse is not always true. Perfor-mance criteria and rewards also differ between the two groups.

The information services department is a highly differentiated spe-cialty; unlike more conventional organizational structures, small task forces are used to design systems. Loosely knit teams in the information services department may work odd hours and may have habits completely different from those of other employees. Role dissatisfaction is common for members of the information services staff; it is very hard to manage computer professionals.

Ambiguities occur in the design and operation of systems. Who is responsible for various problems of input errors or incorrect processing results? Dependence on common resources is also a problem related to the budgeting policies of the organization; the information services de-partment may be seen as taking funds needed by other subunits. Informa-tion services staff members often have personal skills and traits different from those of users; the computer staff generally has a different educa-tional background, interests, and professional orientation.

There are also many communications obstacles between the informa-tion services department and users. Technical jargon can easily confuse users. Another communication problem occurs during systems design when the information services staff attempts to learn user problems. Communications obstacles may prevent the information services staff from understanding how the user works with information and what his needs are for a system.

All these conditions can lead to conflict in the organization. Construc-tive conflict can be productive; however, destructive conflict may make an information system completely ineffective, given the interdependence between the information services department and other subunits. Just as with the transfers of power described earlier, conflict can lead to the for-mation of unfavorable user attitudes. These attitudes result in users refus-ing to cooperate with the design and operation of the information system. Negative attitudes are responsible for many of the extreme user reactions found in the comments section of questionnaires. Feelings have been expressed that the information services department should be eliminated and that many current information systems produce information totally useless to the individuals receiving it.

A DESCRIPTIVE RESEARCH MODEL

Our descriptive model of information systems in the context of the organization in Figure 2.1 has been derived from organizational behavior and information systems literature and studies conducted by the author. The model focuses on three crucial classes of variables: user attitudes and perceptions, the use of systems, and performance. As the model is developed, we present propositions about relationships between the variables in the model and, in subsequent chapters, we test these propositions with emprical data. Many managers would probably regard some of the propositions as self-evident. However, they are stated here for the sake of completeness and to allow us to present supporting data to augment their intuitive appeal.

Variables

The model in Figure 2.1 describes relationships among a number of classes of variables including:

Information services department policies and attitudes
Management actions
User contact and involvement with information systems activities
User attitudes and perceptions of information systems and the information services staff
Technical system quality
Use of a system
User analysis and action
Situational and personal variables
Decision style
Performance

The following discussion states propositions about the relationships among classes of variables. Empirical research to validate these propositions must first identify and operationalize specific variables and then test

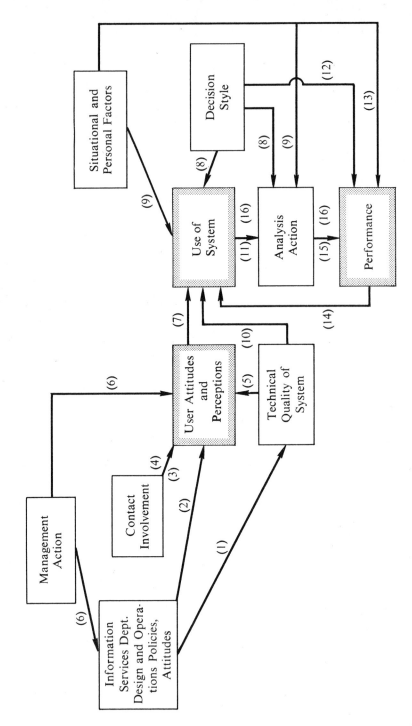

Figure 2.1. A descriptive model of information systems in the context of the organization (the numbers in parentheses refer to propositions in the text).

the relationships among the operationalized variables.* For some of the propositions we can indicate the expected direction of a relationship; in other instances the relationship depends on the specific operational variables of the study.

User Attitudes and Perceptions

The two major groups involved in the design and operation of information systems are the information services department and users. The information services department is responsible for the design of new systems and the operation of existing ones.

Proposition 1. The systems design and operations policies of the information services department and the execution of these policies influence the technical quality of information systems.

The policies and procedures followed by the information services department directly affect technical quality because this group is responsible for systems. By technical quality we mean the extent to which a system works according to specifications and the extent to which an appropriate level of technology has been applied successfully in developing systems. For example, a policy to promote on-line enquiry should result in better systems in terms of less voluminous output and more selective retrieval.

Proposition 2. The systems design and operations policies of the information services department influence user attitudes and perceptions of information systems and the information services staff.

The systems design and operations policies of the information services department also influence attitudes, particularly those of user who are in frequent contact with the department. In working with the department, users form attitudes toward computer systems and the information services staff.

Proposition 3. User contact with information services staff members under adverse conditions leads to unfavorable user attitudes and perceptions of information systems and the information services staff.

* In the next chapter we present the operational variables from each class for the empirical studies discussed in the book.

Contact is generally thought to improve the attitudes between two groups of individuals by increasing understanding. However, when contact occurs under unfavorable conditions, worse attitudes may result. User contact with the information services staff often occurs under adverse conditions when something is wrong, such as an input error or faulty output.

Proposition 4. User involvement in the design and the operation of information systems results in favorable user attitudes and perceptions of information systems and the information services staff.

User involvement has often been suggested as one method to improve the quality and acceptance of information systems (Lucas, 1971, 1973b). These suggestions are based on the benefits of participation in encouraging the acceptance of change, particularly when changes affect work groups (Lawler and Hackman, 1969; Scheflen *et al.*, 1971; Trist, 1963).

Proposition 5. Systems with higher technical quality result in more favorable user attitudes and perceptions of information systems and the information services staff.

From a technological standpoint the information services department has a major influence on the quality of information systems. Users play an important part in design, but the technical success of the system is the responsibility of the information services department. For example, the technical issues of file integrity, program execution, meeting processing schedules, etc., are primarily under the control of the information services department. The quality of systems should influence user attitudes because it is the "product" of the information services department seen by the user.

Proposition 6. High levels of management support for and participation in information systems activities result in favorable information services staff attitudes toward their jobs and users and favorable user attitudes and perceptions of information systems and the information services staff.

Both the information services department and users are influenced by management actions. Unfortunately, management often seems unsure of its role with regard to information systems activities; managers complain that they are unable to evaluate information systems and do not understand the technology. If management actively supports the activities of the information services department, then information services staff members should perceive their jobs to be more important and should have better attitudes. Users should also respond to the leadership of management; if management is active and interested in information systems, then users should be more cooperative and have more favorable attitudes toward information systems activities.

Use of an Information System

Figure 2.1 includes a number of variables which influence the use of an information system. If systems are designed well and have the potential to contribute to the effectiveness of the organization, then management should encourage high levels of use of the system. We have included user performance in the descriptive model because it provides one way to evaluate the use and effectiveness of an information system. A user's performance is influenced by a number of variables, as shown in Figure 2.1.

Proposition 7. Favorable user attitudes and perceptions of information systems and the information services staff lead to high levels of use of an information system.*

User attitudes are expected to be crucial in determining system use. Attitudes have an action component, and favorable attitudes are necessary for high levels of use of a system. If the information services department and the system are regarded unfavorably, it is unlikely that anyone will use the system more than absolutely necessary.

Proposition 8. Individuals with differing decision styles have differing levels of use of information systems, perform different analyses of data, and take different actions based on information.

* We should distinguish here between voluntary and required use. If a decisionmaker has no choice but to use a poorly designed system, high use may be associated with unfavorable attitudes. Favorable attitudes are expected to predict voluntary use.

The decision or cognitive style of the user is also important in determining the use of a system. This class includes a number of variables which relate to differing personal orientations and approaches to decision-making and management. For example, some individuals are not oriented toward using quantitative information. These decisionmakers have a different method (such as intuition) for identifying and solving problems which will be reflected in their use of a system and the action taken. In fact, there is evidence from past research that certain individuals are more data-oriented while others are more intuitive (Doktor and Hamilton, 1973; Mason and Mitroff, 1973).

Proposition 9. Different personal and situational factors lead to differing levels of use of an information system and actions.

In Figure 2.1 it can be seen that situational and personal factors are expected to influence the use of a system too. Personal factors include variables like age and education. A young employee may be more open to technology, whereas a highly educated employee may attempt to apply analytical techniques to the information provided by a system. Situational factors are also important; a new employee may use information to understand his job better. In a sales situation, territory characteristics may be highly important, but in banking the location of the branch and type of customer may determine how an information system is used by bank management.

Personal variables are also important in determining action; for example, older workers may have gained enough knowledge and experience that they take action on less information than younger workers. Similarly the customer base for a retail store or the neighborhood for a branch bank can be expected to influence the action taken on the basis of an information system.

Proposition 10. High levels of system use result from a system with high technical quality.

Technically the quality of a system must be sufficiently high that the system can be used, and it must produce useful information. The user interface is important in design; the mode of presentation for data has to be carefully considered (Mason and Mitroff, 1973.) The use of a system must also favor the best interest of the user. In one case a factory floor data collection system was designed for workers paid on a piece-rate incentive basis. Using the system actually decreased the earnings of the workers, and the system had to be abandoned owing to lack of use and cooperation.

Proposition 11. High levels of use of an information system make it more likely that a user will take action based on the information provided.

Working with the output of an information system can help to define problems and in some cases actually to solve existing problems. However, any resolution of a problem is dependent on the decisionmaker's taking action. The likelihood of action should be associated with high levels of use of the information. First, high levels of use are more likely to show a problem which demands action. Second, a decisionmaker who is likely to take action will probably study information more closely to be sure that he understands the problem and to determine the most appropriate action.

Performance

User performance is influenced by a number of variables, including decision style, personal and situational factors, use of an information system, and action taken based on information.

Proposition 12. Individuals with differing decision styles have differing levels of performance.

The decision style of a user of information systems is expected to affect performance just as it affects system use. A highly analytical individual may perform best in a technical staff position, whereas an intuitive decisionmaker may perform best in a position requiring public contact.

Propostion 13. Different personal and situational factors lead to differing levels of performance.

The situation may dictate appropriate behavior for high performance. For example, a branch bank manager in a small community may act more informally to achieve high performance than a manager in an urban location. Personal factors are also important in performance; an older salesman may outperform a younger man because of his experience acquired over time.

In addition to decision style and personal and situational variables, we expect the use of information systems to be associated with performance. A framework for viewing problems suggested by Pounds (1969) is particularly useful in analyzing this relationship. Pounds distinguishes between problem-finding and problem-solving activities. Problem finding consists in choosing a model of desired conditions and comparing it with reality. The comparison between reality and the desired model is used to generate hypotheses about the nature of the difficulty in an attempt to identify problems. Problem-solving activities are undertaken to eliminate the problem identified during problem finding. Different types of information are needed depending on whether the decisionmaker is in the problem-finding or problem-solving stage.

Proposition 14. Low performance stimulates the use of problem finding information produced by an information system.

The decisionmaker who is aware of his low performance should use any information produced by a system which can help identify problems resulting in low performance. In a field study, Pounds found that the most important problem-finding models in one company were historical. For these historical models, an information system can aid problem finding by calling attention to deviations from past performance, for example by providing data which compare this year's sales with those of last year. A salesman with low performance can use this information to identify problems such as the particular territory or accounts where sales have fallen.

Proposition 15. The use of problem-solving information produced by an information system leads to high levels of performance if the user takes action consistent with the information.

After a problem or series of problems has been identified, the decisionmaker enters the problem-solving stage. Alternative actions are con-

sidered and evaluated, and finally one alternative is selected and implemented. Here the decisionmaker needs information to help evaluate the
consequences of different actions, for example, data to answer "what
if?" questions. Information which helps to implement the chosen action
is also useful. For problem-solving activities it is expected that the use of
information which contributes directly to a decision or to action should
predict high performance. The strength of this association depends on the
decisionmaker's ability to analyze alternatives and to take action consistent with the information, as shown in Figure 2.1.

Proposition 16. For irrelevant information, low levels of use of an information system lead to high performance.

A final case of the relationship between the use of an information system and performance occurs when information provided to the decisionmaker is irrelevant. This situation corresponds to information overload described by Ackoff (1967). In this case the use of information
detracts from other problem-finding and problem-solving activities and is
dysfunctional. Low levels of use of the information system should predict
high performance under these conditions. The decisionmaker should not
spend his time analyzing irrelevant data.

Predictions

If the propositions and model are valid, we can easily see why there
have been so many organizational behavior problems in the design and
operation of information systems. Consider the following scenario: First,
the information services department ignores changes in user jobs and
work relationships in designing new systems and implements systems in a
highly authoritarian manner. The department ignores power transfers and
the frustrations users may encounter with a foreign and poorly understood
technology. Systems are operated in the same manner; users are blamed
for errors and the information services department is unresponsive to
requests for changes and does not follow schedules.

Meantime, management does not influence information services department activities, but instead leaves its management to technical specialists.
Management furnishes no leadership for users who judge that information
systems are not important in the organization. According to the model,
practices of the information services department influence user attitudes.

Poor attitudes will reduce cooperation; users will not encourage the design of new systems and will tend to sabotage existing ones. Owing to badly designed systems, little or no user input, and poor attitudes, systems will not be used unless mandatory, for example, if a system is the only way to process the payroll. Information systems will have little or no influence on user performance. In this situation, information systems have failed because their contribution to the organization is nonexistent or far below potential. Given these conditions, new systems will not have a chance for success and a cycle of continued failure can be expected.

If the results of empirical research validate our propositions, the model and results can be used to help reverse this scenario. We will be able to suggest actions to improve user attitudes and perceptions of information systems and the information services staff. Techniques for producing systems that are used and that contribute to organizational performance should emerge from the research.

PAST RESEARCH

Most past research has not been directly concerned with our primary interest: the development and operation of successful information systems. These earlier studies have tended to deal with the impact of systems on the structure of the organization or on changes in employment levels after the introduction of a computer.

Organizational Structure

Early predictions about the impact of computers on organizations suggested that there would be increased centralization as a result of computer systems (Leavitt and Whisler, 1958). Computers would let top management regain control over the organization and remove one motivation for decentralization. A restructuring of management levels was expected. However, one study found little evidence of the impact of computers on centralization in the insurance industry (Whisler and Meyer, 1967).

Work Roles

Reductions in personnel also provided an early interest in the study of the impact of computers on organizations. Changes in middle management jobs were predicted by Leavitt and Whisler (1958). There is some evidence that decisionmaking is moving to higher levels in the organization and becoming more quantitative as a result of computer systems, at least in the insurance industry (Whisler and Meyer, 1967). For non-management employees, research suggests some increases in the skill levels required and more pressure from deadlines after computer systems have been installed (Whisler and Meyer, 1967).

Specific Systems

The studies reported above have generally examined the impact of all systems in the organization, using cross-sectional data. This research design makes it difficult to demonstrate that changes were caused by computer system activities; however, there have been several studies of the impact of a single system. One early case study of the implementation of a system described a number of problems and negative employee reactions; this study points out the importance of organizational problems in the implementation of a system (Mann and Williams, 1960). Another study in the insurance industry found that employees felt that the conversion to a computer system had a relatively minor impact on them (Hardin, 1960). Two researchers examined the installation of computer systems in British banks in some detail and found that employees who differed on personal variables like age and sex had different reactions to new systems (Mumford and Banks, 1967).

Conclusions

The early studies of the gross impact of computer systems are not too helpful in suggesting ways to design and operate information systems more effectively. Of the studies described above, only those concerned with implementation of a single system are really useful in forecasting the impact of a system and learning better ways to manage information system activities (Hardin, 1960; Mann and Williams, 1960; Mumford and Banks, 1967). Unfortunately, the research summarized above was conducted in a relatively small number of industries and all of the studies are fairly old. Early systems did not encompass as many departments as today's systems, and most of the early systems were transactional in nature, providing little information for decisionmaking.

The early studies do furnish some background, but their contribution to the research described in this book is small. The data presented here are drawn from more contemporary systems and from a variety of companies and industries. The model in Figure 2.1 and the studies in the next chapters are concerned with the design and operation of effective information systems and their use within the context of the organization. The three chapters on results (4 through 6) discuss variables associated with user attitudes and perceptions, the use of an information system, and user performance, respectively.

THREE

the research studies

INTRODUCTION

IN THIS CHAPTER we describe the studies used to test the propositions of the descriptive model. We delineate the operational variables in each of the studies, and the results presented in the next three chapters refer to these variables. Letter symbols are used to identify an operational variable, the letter designating the class of the variable; for example, an "A" refers to an attitudinal variable. Each symbol has two subscripts; the first identifies the study (from 1 to 6 in the order presented in this chapter), and the second represents a particular operational variable in the study. Operational variables are defined in a table accompanying the description of each of the studies. While specific operational variables differ among the studies, the operational variables are representative of the variable classes in the model, given the unique environment of each study.

Each study included a questionnaire as one method of collecting data. The format of the majority of the questions on the questionnaire consisted of a seven-point scale on which the respondent circled a number to indicate his response. For example:

My general impression of the computer staff is that they are:

| Not too competent technically | 1 2 3 4 5 6 7 | Highly competent technically |

This type of question can be answered quickly and makes it more likely that a respondent will complete the entire questionnaire. For the few questions where this format was inappropriate, the questionnaire used fill-in-the-blank or multiple-choice items.

Several questions were applicable to all of the studies; however, in each study a significant portion of the questionnaire was developed explicitly for the organization(s) involved. Correlations and factor analytic techniques were used to combine items from each questionnaire into scales. That is, several items which were highly related and appeared to measure the same variable were averaged together to increase measurement reliability. In general, for all the variables in the studies, higher numerical values represent more favorable responses (for example, higher sales, more favorable attitudes, etc.). Table 3.1 summarizes the six studies and provides an overview of the detailed discussions which follow.

1. THE SIX-COMPANY STUDY

Background
The first research study to be discussed was conducted as part of the requirements for the author's doctoral dissertation at MIT (Lucas, 1974b). This study was exploratory in nature; past work had not dealt with the relationship between user attitudes and information services department (ISD) activities. It was necessary first to define key variables and develop some means for measuring them. The original goal was to determine the differences between firms under facilities management and those under internal management of the information services department.* However, the results from all the firms turned out to be more significant than differences among companies, based on the type of management.

The study included six firms in three industries: style merchandise manufacturing, food processing, and mail order sales. One firm in each of the three industries had a facilities management contract and the other one operated its information services department internally. All firms had mature computer operations; a number of systems had been implemented

---

* In facilities management a consulting firm executes a contract to assume the management of the information services department of a client organization.

Table 3.1. Characteristics of the Studies

Study	Type	Sample	Number of Subjects	Data Collection Date
1. Six-Company	Field	Users in 6 firms in 3 industries	683	1969
2. Bay Area	Field	Users in 7 manu-facturing firms	616	1971
3. University	Field	Users of administrative computing across numerous departments	117	1973
4. Sales Force	Field	Retail salesmen in one apparel company	419	1972
5. Branch Bank	Field	Branch bank managers and assistant manag-ers for a large California bank	316	1972
6. Experiment	Laboratory	MBA candidates and executives	115	1973
Totals		16 companies, 1 labora-tory experiment	2266	4 years

and others were under development. All the systems involved in the study were batch-processing in nature. The sample consisted of 683 users in the 6 companies, ranging from vice presidents to clerks in all departments having some contact with the information services department.

Variables

A questionnaire was devised for the study and was pretested prior to collection of final data. The questionnaire itself was administered on the job with a covering letter from a company official. The variables derived from the questionnaire are shown in Table 3.2. Computer potential was measured in the study by two items on the questionnaire concerning the clerical and managerial decisionmaking potential of computer systems. Attitudes toward the information services department staff were measured by a scale including a number of items describing the staff, ranging from its technical competence to the quality of systems design, training, and the ability of the staff to deal with people.

The perceived quality-of-service scale was derived from several items

Table 3.2. Variables from the Six Company Study

Variable Class	Symbol [a]	Description	Source
User attitudes	A_{11}	Computer potential	Questionnaire
	A_{12}	Attitudes toward the information services department staff	Questionnaire
User perceptions	V_{11}	Perceived quality of Information services department service	Questionnaire
	V_{12}	Perceived management support	Questionnaire
	V_{13}	Perceived involvement in designing systems	Questionnaire
	V_{14}	Week's contact with EDP	Questionnaire

[a] The first subscript of each symbol refers to the study and the second to the variable within the study.

describing input and output. Input questions included ease of preparation, accuracy, ease of corrections, and the degree of duplication for input data. Output was described according to its timeliness, detail, accuracy, legibility, and general usefulness.

Perceived management support was measured by a single item on the questionnaire which asked the degree to which the respondent felt management supported continued computer operations in the firm. Involvement consisted of two items: the user's perception of the amount of involvement, and the length of time spent working on a computer project. Contact was measured by a question on how much time the respondent had spent working on information systems department activities during the preceding week.

2. THE BAY AREA STUDY

Background

To extend the results of the Six-Company study, a survey of seven San Francisco Bay Area manufacturing firms was undertaken (Lucas, 1973c). In the first study all the variables were developed from the questionnaire except the distinction between facilities management and internal management of the information services department. It is possible that all the responses are due to a "halo" effect from the questionnaire; that is, variables are associated because respondents with favorable attitudes marked all items high and vice versa. In the Bay Area study we used independent sources of data and extended the earlier results by including a larger number of variables.

Seven firms manufacturing a range of products from computers to food stuffs participated in the study. All of these firms had medium to large scale computers and an active information services department staff. Only two of the systems in different companies were on-line; the bulk of the systems involved were batch-processing in nature. A total of 616 users completed a modified version of the questionnaire used in the original Six-Company study. (The modified questionnaire was pretested.) The survey was distributed on the job and the information services department manager in each firm was interviewed to collect data on systems design and operations policies.

Variables

Two sets of variables were developed in the study: information services department policies and user attitudes and perceptions (see Table 3.3). The attitudinal variables are very similar to those developed in the first study; for example, the measurement of computer potential and attitudes toward the information services department staff are similar to the corresponding variables in the Six-Company study. In the Bay Area study, ratings of the quality of input and output were scored separately. Input quality consisted of ratings of the ease of preparation, ease of correction, accuracy, and amount of duplication of input data. Ratings of the output quality included timeliness, detail, accuracy, legibility, ease of changing the output, and general usefulness of reports.

Perceived management support indicates how much the user feels that management of the firm supports more use of computers. The training variable consists of two items concerned with the user's perceptions of the amount of training received and how well prepared he feels when a new system is implemented. Involvement includes items describing the length of time the user spent working on a systems development project and the extent of his involvement.

A number of information services department policies were discussed during the interviews with department managers. The first variable in-

Table 3.3. Variables in the Bay Area Study

Variable Class	Symbol [a]	Description	Source
User attitudes	A_{21}	Computer potential	Question-naire
	A_{22}	Attitude toward information services department staff	Question-naire
User percep-tions	V_{21}	Perceived quality of input	Question-naire
	V_{22}	Perceived quality of output	Question-naire
	V_{23}	Perceived management support	Question-naire
	V_{24}	Perceived involvement in designing systems	Question-naire
	V_{25}	Perceived training received	Question-naire
ISD operations policies	O_{21}	Reporting level of infor-mation services department manager	Interview
	O_{22}	Use of computer steering committee	Interview
	O_{23}	Method of charging for services	Interview
	O_{24}	Presence of a user representative	Interview
ISD systems design policies	C_{21}	Primary source of systems	Interview
	C_{22}	Primary source of changes	Interview
	C_{23}	Use of file management packages	Interview
	C_{24}	Presence of on-line systems	Interview
	C_{25}	Mean number of reports produced	Interview

[a] The first subscript of each symbol refers to the study and the second to the variable in the study.

dicates whether the manager of the information services department reports to the vice presidential level or above. Another variable measures whether or not a steering committee is in use in the company. The information services department managers also indicated whether users were charged directly for services or whether computer expenses were all charged to overhead. Finally, the managers reported the presence of any user representatives, that is, individuals designated within the information services department to act as representatives for users with problems or suggestions.

A number of systems design policies differed from company to company in the study. The first variable distinguishes whether the primary source of new systems is the information services staff or users. The same question was asked for the source of changes to existing systems. Another variable indicates the use of file management packages to provide greater flexibility for users. The presence or absence of any on-line systems is another systems design variable.

For six of the firms in the Bay Area study, data were available on the number of reports produced by three major systems * (Lucas, 1974a). These data provided a measure of the mean number of reports produced by the systems within each company.

3. THE UNIVERSITY STUDY

Background

A study of administrative computing services in a major university was undertaken. The university administrative computer staff had developed a number of batch systems in such areas as accounting, payroll, employee data, student and alumni records. In addition, an on-line system which served a number of administrative functions was being implemented at the time of the study. Users participated in a questionnaire survey through interdepartmental mail to determine the level of use of systems and user attitudes and perceptions of computer services. Approximately 70% (117) of the relevant individuals responded to the questionnaire (Lucas, 1974d).

One of the goals of the study was to develop an independent rating of systems quality, and a separate questionnaire was administered for this purpose to one to three information service department staff members having contact with each of the 26 systems in use. The questionnaire forced an evaluation based on user-oriented criteria rather than on the technical elegance or sophistication of the system. We attempted to have at least two people on the information services department staff rate each

* With the exception of one of the six firms where only two systems could be included.

system, and the results for each system were averaged to form a score for each variable.

The scales on the user questionnaire were quite similar to those of the two earlier studies. User respondents also indicated each of the 26 systems which they used in some capacity. To develop a single rating by the information service department staff for each user, the department ratings were averaged for each of the systems used. Thus the independent variables which rate service quality are averages for each variable of the information services department staff evaluation for all the systems with which the user reported having contact.

Variables

The variables in the study are shown in Table 3.4. The variables labeled "ISD ratings" were derived by the process described above from the questionnaire administered to the information services department staff; all other variables were developed from the user questionnaire.

The questionnaire completed by the information services department staff provided seven scales evaluating the quality of information systems. Input and output quality are based on the clarity of input/output documents, input error ratings, and the usefulness, accuracy, and timeliness of output reports. The overall quality-of-systems scale consists of ratings of system flexibility, the lack of pressure to reprogram the system, and the completeness of the functions contained in the system.

An analysis of the staff questionnaire indicated that questions on the integration of systems and on the lack of change requests should be combined into a single variable (R_{34}). Systems usefulness consists of a rating of how much the system can be used for decisionmaking (analysis, planning, taking action, and problem finding). Documentation, training, and systems accuracy also form a single scale (variable R_{36}). Finally, for online systems the rating scale consists of items reflecting the response time and the stability of the system.

The user questionnaire contributed several situational and personal variables. Position refers to the level of the respondent in the organization and ranges from clerical workers to top management. Time on the job represents the length of time the respondent has been in his present position. The questionnaire also furnishes age and education data.

For batch systems, two scales were derived from the user questionnaire to measure the amount of use of information systems. The first variable

Table 3.4. Variables in the University Study

Variable Class	Symbol [a]	Description	Source
ISD ratings	R_{31}	Input quality	ISD staff questionnaire
	R_{32}	Output quality	ISD staff questionnaire
	R_{33}	Overall quality	ISD staff questionnaire
	R_{34}	Integration and changes requested	ISD staff questionnaire
	R_{35}	System usefulness	ISD staff questionnaire
	R_{36}	Documentation, training, accuracy	ISD staff questionnaire
	R_{37}	On-line performance	ISD staff questionnaire
Situational	S_{31}	Position	User questionnaire
	S_{32}	Time on job	User questionnaire
Personal	I_{31}	Education	User questionnaire
	I_{32}	Age	User questionnaire
Use of system	U_{31}	Batch system amount of use	User questionnaire
	U_{32}	Batch use for various activities/decisions	User questionnaire
	U_{33}	On-line system use of specific features	User questionnaire
	U_{34}	On-line system use in general	User questionnaire
User attitudes	A_{31}	Computer potential	User questionnaire
	A_{32}	Attitudes toward ISD Staff	User questionnaire
User perceptions	V_{31}	Input quality	User questionnaire
	V_{32}	Output quality	User questionnaire
	V_{33}	Rating of on-line system	User questionnaire
	V_{34}	Training	User questionnaire
	V_{35}	Contact with information services department	User questionnaire
	V_{36}	Management support	User questionnaire
	V_{37}	Suitability of number of reports received	User questionnaire
	V_{38}	Would like more summary and exception reports	User questionnaire
	V_{39}	Involvement	User questionnaire

[a] The first subscript in each symbol refers to the study and the second to the variable in the study.

(U_{31}) deals with general use of batch systems. The second variable (U_{32}) is concerned with the use of batch systems for specific functions like decisionmaking and trend analysis. The questionnaire analysis provided two usage scales for on-line systems. The first one (U_{33}) is concerned with the frequency of use of the on-line system and the use of specific functions like the enquiry language. The second usage scale (U_{34}) represents use of the on-line system for different activities, like decisionmaking and trend analysis.

User attitudes toward information systems (computer potential and attitudes toward the information services department staff) were measured by the same variables as in the two earlier studies. The University study also includes a number of user perceptions of information services department activities. Ratings of input and output quality are similar to those described for the Bay Area study. Ratings of the on-line system include an evaluation of its response time, reliability, and ease of use.

The training scale is similar to the corresponding Bay Area study variable. Contact with the information services department was measured by an item on which the respondent indicated the amount of time spent on information systems–related activities during the preceding week. Perceived management support is a single item on the questionnaire reflecting the user's perception of the extent to which management supports more administrative computer use within the university.

A high response on the scale for the suitability of the number of reports received indicates that the user is satisfied with the reports he receives at present or that he would like to receive even more reports from the computer. On the other hand, a high score on the desire for summary and exception reports means that the user would like to receive more reports of this type, while a low score indicates that he is relatively satisfied with the present form of reports. Involvement includes two items from the questionnaire reflecting the extent and the length of time the respondent has been involved in designing new information systems.

4. THE SALES FORCE STUDY

Background
The company involved in this study is a major manufacturer of ready-to-wear clothing (Lucas, 1975a). The firm employs a large sales

force calling on retailers, who in turn sell to the buying public. The sales force is divided into two groups; account executives handle from one to six accounts and are the most highly paid. Sales representatives constitute the bulk of the sales force and average from sixty accounts in one division to over a hundred in another. The sales force is paid by commission, and a higher rate is in effect for sales above target.

Three major divisions in the company participated in the study; Division A is the oldest and sells the original product manufactured by the company. The particular product sold in Division A is relatively insensitive to style or fashion considerations; the company can sell all that its production facilities are capable of manufacturing. Sales have been increasing in this division and sales representatives have been in their position and territory longer on the average than representatives in the other divisions. For purposes of data analysis, the largest division was divided into two groups: a 60% estimation and a 40% validation sample.*

Division B is the newest one in the company and was formed to sell sportswear. These clothes are more fashion-sensitive than the product sold by Division A, but the division is staffed primarily with salesmen who worked in Division A before the organization of Division B. This division had the smallest bookings increase during the year and had existed for only a short while at the time the study was undertaken. Division C specializes in the sale of fashion clothing for women and faces the most uncertain environment; style and fashion considerations create a more volatile market and a greater sales challenge.

The company is a major user of computers and has numerous applications, including the sales information system of the study. The objective of the system is to support the activities of the sales force by providing its members with complete data on their accounts. The system was originally planned in the 1960s and has evolved over time on the basis of feedback from the sales force and management. Input to the system comes from orders submitted by sales representatives and the output of a computer-based shipping system.

The major output of the sales system is a monthly report which provides total sales activity data on a year-to-date basis for each account assigned to a member of the sales force. The sales system maintains de-

---

* Results are first estimated using 60% of the sample. Then the remaining 40% of the data are processed using the relationships estimated at first to validate the results.

tailed data on sales to each buying entity by product line. (A buying entity is a customer location from which an order can be placed, for example, the sportswear section of the men's department in a clothing store.) The output report for each sales force member's account shows the data for the past 12 months on units shipped and cancellations and the bookings for the next 4 months. Dollar sales figures are provided, as is a this-year-to-date, last-year-to-date comparison. Summary totals are produced by department, store, and account (one account may have multiple stores). Detailed data are distributed to sales representatives, while some detailed information plus regional and district summaries are sent to sales management. The 35,000-page sales report is distributed among the sales force and management each month.

A sales force member can use the report in a number of ways, for example, to locate inadequate bookings by line or an inadequate product mix. The recipient can examine the pattern of bookings and shipment data for this year versus last year and study cancellations in relation to bookings. Comparisons between aggregate bookings to date this year and last year provide a benchmark for evaluating progress during the current year. The sales force member can also use the report to identify dormant and inactive accounts and to allocate sales efforts and plan calls.

Variables

Table 3.5 shows the specific variables included in the Sales Force study. Collection of data took several forms, including an analysis of computer files and the administration of a questionnaire to salesmen and account executives; and there was a 90% return after one follow-up. (The questionnaire was distributed through company mail and returned through the U.S. mails.)

The performance variable used in this study was gross bookings for the 1972 selling season; it was obtained from the sales information system files. (Several other performance variables were considered, but gross bookings appeared to be the best indicator available.)

Two situational factors, the number of accounts and an approximation of the number of buying entities, were obtained from the sales information system computer files. Both length of time in the present territory and position, measured in months, came from the questionnaire. Personnel records provided data on age and education.

Questions about the use of information on the major report provided by

Table 3.5. Variables in the Sales Force Study

Variable Class	Symbol [a]	Description	Source
Performance	P_{41}	Total dollar bookings 1972 season	Computer files
Situational	S_{41}	Number of accounts	Computer files
	S_{42}	Number of buying entities (approximate)	Computer files
	S_{43}	Length of time in present territory (months)	Questionnaire
	S_{44}	Length of time in present position (months)	Questionnaire
Personal	I_{41}	Age	Personnel records
	I_{42}	Education	Personnel records
Use of system	U_{41}	Working with customer in store	Questionnaire
	U_{42}	Detailed analysis of buying entity (account)	Questionnaire
	U_{43}	Overall progress [b]	Questionnaire
	U_{44}	Summary this year versus last	Questionnaire
	U_{45}	Planning	Questionnaire
	U_{46}	Cancellations	Questionnaire
Decision style	$D_{41}{}^{c}$	Records orientation—keeps own item records	Questionnaire
	$D_{42}{}^{c}$	Calculations performed with sales report data	Questionnaire
User attitudes	A_{41}	Computer potential	Questionnaire
User perceptions	V_{41}	Quality of output	Questionnaire
	V_{42}	Management computer support	Questionnaire

[a] The first subscript of each symbol refers to the study and the second to the variables in the study.
[b] Divisions A and B only.   [c] Dummy variables.

the sales information system from the questionnaire were factor-analyzed for each division. Because the results of the factor analysis were similar for divisions A and B, the same scales were constructed for each division. As Division C produced slightly different factors, several of its scales consist of different items from the questionnaire. However, the scales have roughly the same identity for all divisions.

One group of items from the questionnaire was combined to form a scale which describes the respondent using the sales report in the store with customers. A second usage scale includes questionnaire items dealing with the detailed examination of data for a buying entity. Another scale was formed from questions which relate to planning and general problem finding, such as planning calls and subdividing a territory for travel purposes. The overall progress scale reflects the use of information on bookings and shipments for this year and last year. A general summary scale includes items comparing this year's and last year's performance for actual bookings and percentage changes. Several items on the questionnaire formed a scale related to planning activities. The scale on cancellations represents use of sections of the report describing returns and allowances.

Two questions on the questionnaire are included in the decision style category. Each respondent indicated whether he kept his own records at the item level (the sales information system reports on lines, not items) and whether he performed any calculations of his own with the information on the report. These two questions are rough indicators of the respondent's orientation toward keeping records and performing computations.

Attitudes and perceptions of computer systems in general were obtained from the questionnaire, and they follow very closely the scales for the three studies discussed earlier. Computer potential is measured by two questions on the potential of computers in sales work and managerial decisionmaking. The output quality scale is analogous to the one used in the Bay Area study. Perceived management support is measured by two questions about the respondent's perception of the degree to which both general management and his immediate superior support more use of the computer in sales work.

5. THE BRANCH BANK STUDY

Background

The organization involved in this study is a major California bank with over 200 branches in the state. Branch banking in California is unique; there is intense competition even for retail business, which is often ignored by commercial banks in other states. Each branch is staffed by a manager, an assistant manager, and an operations staff whose size varies with the volume of business at the branch. The manager of the branch is responsible for all of its operations and he is supervised by a division manager.

Each officer has authorized loan limits and must secure permission from the division loan supervision department to exceed them. The branch lending officers do, however, have certain latitude in negotiating with customers to meet competition. Generally, the assistant manager of the branch handles the day-to-day operational problems, and the manager concentrates on loans and customer relations. (In extremely small branches the manager may be more involved in operations and may spend less time working with customers.) The bank maintains statistics of branch performance which include five key indicators: the volume of commercial loans, of installment loans, of real estate loans, and the size of demand deposit checking accounts and savings balances.

The bank in this study is a major user of computers and has a number of formal information systems producing reports for distribution to branch management. Interviews were held with members of the information system department staff to select reports which have managerial significance, that is, which provide information beyond routine transactional data. The research focused on four major reports sent to branch managers. (When finished with the reports, most branch managers send them to their assistant managers for review.)

The first report in the study deals with branch objectives. The bank has instituted a goal performance system in which points are awarded for achieving yearly goals. This particular report shows the actual and projected branch performance, the yearly goal, the point value, and points earned for demand deposits, individual savings, commercial loans, real estate loans, and installment loans.

The second report in the study is called ''the monthly profit summary.'' It displays the earnings of all deposits and loans made by the branch and provides a summary of direct expenses. Profit for the year-to-date, projected profits, and percentage of projected profits achieved are all shown on the report. Branch management can use these two reports to determine how they are progressing toward achieving the yearly goals of the branch. It is also possible to analyze the reports to show which deposits and loans are the most profitable.

Table 3.6. Variables in the Branch Bank Study

Variable Class	Symbol [a]	Description	Source
Performance	P_{51}	Weighted actual performance 1972	Computer files
	P_{52}	Adjusted percentage of commercial loan goal 1972	Computer files
	P_{53}	Adjusted percentage of installment loan goal 1972	Computer files
	P_{54}	Adjusted percentage of real estate loan goal 1972	Computer files
	P_{55}	Adjusted percentage of demand deposit accounts goal 1972	Computer files
	P_{56}	Adjusted percentage of savings goal 1972	Computer files
	P_{57}	Supervisor rating	Questionnaire
Situational	S_{51}	High potential location [b]	Computer files
	S_{52}	Static location [b]	Computer files
	S_{53}	Moderate potential location [b]	Computer files
	S_{54}	Stable customer base [b]	Computer files
	S_{55}	Transitional customer base [b]	Computer files
	S_{56}	Hub office competition [b]	Computer files
	S_{57}	Heavy competition [b]	Computer files
	S_{58}	Light competition [b]	Computer files
Personal	I_{51}	Age	Questionnaire
	I_{52}	Years at bank	Questionnaire
	I_{53}	Years in position	Questionnaire
	I_{54}	Years at branch	Questionnaire
	I_{55}	Education	Questionnaire
Use of reports	U_{51}	Branch objectives	Questionnaire
	U_{52}	Monthly profit summary	Questionnaire
	U_{53}	Monthly deposit, loan balance and income/expense report	Questionnaire

The third major report examined in the study is the monthly deposit, loan balance, and income expense report. This report shows the deposits and loan balance for each type of account for each month. The fourth major report is a daily statement, a detailed balance sheet for the branch. The latter two reports provide information on current activities and can be used by management as a check on operations and for analyzing day-to-day problems.

Variable Class	Symbol [a]	Description	Source
Use of reports (continued)	U_{54}	Daily statement	Questionnaire
	U_{55}	Enquiry system	Questionnaire
Decision style	D_{51}	Keeps own records [b]	Questionnaire
	D_{52}	Number of customer calls (weekly)	Questionnaire
	D_{53}	Activism	Questionnaire
	D_{54}	Makes exceptions on limits	Questionnaire
	D_{55}	Needs approvals	Questionnaire
	D_{56}	Scans report [b]	Questionnaire
	D_{57}	Looks for exceptions on report [b]	Questionnaire
	D_{58}	Reads summary information on report [b]	Questionnaire
	D_{59}	Studies report in detail [b]	Questionnaire
		Call to the Attention of Other Employees	
Action	E_{51}	Monthly profit summary	Questionnaire
	E_{52}	Monthly deposit, loan balance and income/expense report	Questionnaire
	E_{53}	Daily statement	Questionnaire
		Reallocate Branch Efforts	
	E_{54}	Branch objectives	Questionnaire
	E_{55}	Monthly profit summary	Questionnaire
	E_{56}	Monthly deposit, loan balance and income/expense report	Questionnaire
User perceptions	V_{51}	Output quality	Questionnaire
	V_{52}	Involvement in setting goals	Questionnaire
	V_{53}	Compensation based on goals	Questionnaire

[a] The first subscript of each symbol refers to the study and the second to the variables in the study.
[b] Dummy variables.

Variables

The variables in this study are shown in Table 3.6. Data, collected from several sources, included a questionnaire administered by mail to managers and assistant managers of 165 branches in three divisions of the bank. The response with one follow-up for the questionnaire was 96% for managers and 95% for assistant managers.* In addition to the question-

* A number of the responses being incomplete, the sample size for analyses involving certain variables was reduced.

naire sent to branch management, division managers also filled out one that rated the branch and assistant branch managers in their own division.* Data were also available from computer files maintained by the information services department and management sciences staff.

The performance variable, P_{51}, represents an index of actual 1972 performance weighted by the points assigned in the branch objectives system for each indicator (commercial loans, installment loans, etc.). The performance indicators, P_{52} through P_{55}, represent the adjusted percentage of each branch goal achieved for the 1972 year.

An extensive study conducted earlier by the management sciences staff showed that a number of situational variables affect growth in demand deposit accounts and savings balances. (Both of these balances are probably the least subject to management influence and the most dependent on external factors like customer base or branch location.) Regressions were run using the situational factors in Table 3.6 to predict the absolute percentage of 1972 goals achieved by each branch. The percentage of the goal achieved for each indicator was then adjusted in an attempt to factor out the effects of the situational variables. The adjusted performance indicators, P_{52} through P_{56}, should reflect the efforts of managers and assistant managers more accurately than unadjusted figures. Finally, variable P_{57} represents the division manager's ratings of the branch manager.

The situational variables in the study are those developed by the management sciences staff as described above. The staff classified each branch on the potential of its location (high, static, moderate), customer base (stable, transitional), and degree of competition (hub office, heavy, light).

Personal factors on age, education, and length of time with the bank, in this position and at the branch, were taken directly from the questionnaire. Several decision style variables also came from the questionnaire. The respondent indicated whether he kept records of his own and estimated the average number of calls he made on customers each week. Variables D_{53} through D_{55} were developed through factor analysis; each variable is a scale representing several items from the questionnaire. Activism includes bank management working with the client, for example, to restructure loans. Limits and exceptions refer to the percentage of

* Assistant manager ratings could not be included because one division manager was unable to provide them.

loans which branch management makes in excess of its limits. Needing approval is an estimate of the percentage of loans to be approved by division loan supervision.

Scales describing the use of the formal information system were developed from items on the questionnaire about the use of specific information on the reports. Factor analytic and correlation techniques showed that all of these items could be included in a single usage scale for each report. Action taken on the basis of the information in the reports falls into two categories representing the likelihood that branch management will call the attention of another employee to a problem or that it will attempt to reallocate branch efforts.

Output quality was measured by a series of items on the questionnaire similar to those used in the Bay Area study. Perceived involvement in this study is related to participation setting branch goals rather than the development of information systems. Finally, the last variable measures the extent to which a respondent feels his compensation is based on achieving branch goals.

6. THE EXPERIMENT

Background

A laboratory experiment was conducted to examine differences in performance resulting from the use of different information and different methods of presenting information. The experiment included a variety of treatments, for example, teletype hard copy versus CRT tabular displays versus CRT graphical displays. The experiment utilized a transportation management game in which a player decides on the amount of a product to be shipped from a West Coast manufacturing plant to an East Coast distribution center and on the mode of transportation for the shipments.

The player has to control inventory and warehouse space in the East and faces an unknown demand function. The carriers have expected arrival times which vary according to a probability distribution that is unknown to the player. The game is similar to a number of decisionmaking situations in logistics, production control, manufacturing, etc.

Shipping decisions are entered for four weeks at a time by each player. At the completion of a four-week period the reports described below are produced and input is prepared for the next four-week period. For experimental purposes the game was modified to run on a time-sharing computer system. Each player competes only against four computerized phantom teams following uniquely predetermined strategies in each play. Each player's results are completely independent of other players' actions.

The information system for the game consists of four major reports; the form and presentation of several additional reports were varied during the experiment. (The following four reports were received by each player regardless of the experimental treatment.) The current status of shipments report is used to show what has been shipped, what has arrived, and what is scheduled to arrive by each carrier. The inventory position report shows beginning inventory, sales, arrivals, and ending inventory. The profit-and-loss statement is a complete breakdown of sales and expenses. A statistics report provides summary sales, costs, and profit data. (Certain information on this report was supplemented in some of the experimental treatments with industry results, industry production, GNP figures, etc.)

Three major experimental groups were involved in the study. A group of 36 Stanford Graduate School of Business MBA candidates formed the first set of players; another 36 players were utility company executives attending an Industrial Engineering (IE) summer program at Stanford. The last group consisted of 43 executives in the Stanford Summer Executive Program (SEP).

The subjects played two sessions, the first being treated as a learning session. All subjects started in the same position for a second session, and the results for the second period were used in the analysis. To motivate the players, prizes were awarded for the highest profit for the combined sessions. All subjects completed a questionnaire on the use of the reports and a test on decision style at the end of the experiment.

Variables

The variables in the experiment which are relevant for our purposes are shown in Table 3.7. The performance variables P_{61} through P_{65} are the player's profits during each month of the second session alone, and P_{67} is the total profit for the second period. One decision style variable is a continuous score derived from the Sensing-Intuition scale of the Myers-Briggs psychological test. A high value on this score indicates a more intuitive, and a low value a more sensing or analytic, approach to problem solving.

Table 3.7. Variables in the Experiment

Variable Class	Symbol [a]	Description	Source
Performance	P_{61}	Profits in month 1	Computer records
	P_{62}	Profits in month 2	Computer records
	P_{63}	Profits in month 3	Computer records
	P_{64}	Profits in month 4	Computer records
	P_{65}	Profits in month 5	Computer records
	P_{67}	Total profits, session 2	Computer records
Decision style	D_{61}	Sensing versus intuitive Decisionmaking	Questionnaire
Use	U^C_{61}	General use current status of shipments report (CSS)	Questionnaire
	U^C_{62}	Blocked space/leased warehouse (CSS)	Questionnaire
	U^C_{63}	Verify shipment (CSS)	Questionnaire
	U^C_{64}	Value (CSS)	Questionnaire
	U^I_{61}	Audit inventory using inventory position report (IP)	Questionnaire
	U^I_{62}	Select carrier (IP)	Questionnaire
	U^I_{63}	Value (IP)	Questionnaire
	U^I_{64}	Develop strategy (IP)	Questionnaire
	U^I_{65}	Inventory control (IP)	Questionnaire
	U^I_{66}	Locate inventory problem (IP)	Questionnaire
	U^I_{66}	Find problem (IP)	Questionnaire
	U^P_{61}	General use profit and loss statement (PL)	Questionnaire
	U^P_{62}	Uncontrollable costs (PL)	Questionnaire
	U^P_{63}	Controllable costs (PL)	Questionnaire
	U^P_{64}	Blocked space/leased warehouse (PL)	Questionnaire
	U^S_{61}	Value of statistical and economic indicators report (SE)	Questionnaire
	U^S_{62}	Problem finding (SE)	Questionnaire
	G_{61}	Demand graph	CRT monitor
	G_{62}	Closing inventory graph	CRT monitor
	G_{63}	Sales graph	CRT monitor
	G_{64}	Industry sales graph	CRT monitor
	G_{65}	GNP graph	CRT monitor
	G_{66}	GNP forecast graph	CRT monitor
	G_{67}	Production index graph	CRT monitor
	G_{68}	Production index forecast graph	CRT monitor
	G_{69}	Demand for substitute product graph	CRT monitor

[a] The first subscript of each symbol refers to the study and the second to the variable in the study. The superscript on the usage variables refers to the report containing the data, for example U^C_{61} is general use current status of shipment report (CSS).

A number of usage scales were derived from the questionnaire for each of the basic reports provided to all groups. These reports include the current status of shipments, which can be used to determine what has been shipped and what has arrived. The report also can be used to determine how much space to block (a guaranteed minimum air shipment each week which is billed whether used or not) and how much warehouse space to lease (extra space on a lease basis is cheaper than resorting to public warehouses to store excess inventories). Users also rated the value of the current status of shipments report.

The inventory position report is used to audit inventory, and it might be helpful in selecting a carrier. The report can be used to develop a playing strategy, find general problems, locate inventory problems, and for inventory control. Players also rated the value of the inventory position report.

The profit and loss statement is used to examine controllable and uncontrollable costs; it also provides information on blocked space and leased warehouse expenses. A statistical and economic indicators report provides data on trends and for problem finding.

The final set of usage variables were developed from a monitor which recorded the use of data items for the graphics treatments in the experiment. All the graphics displays were cumulative from the beginning of the session to the last input. Each time a player in one of the graphics groups requested a display, the data item graphed was recorded for that period. (Of course, this measure only means that the information was displayed, and does not indicate whether or not the information was actually used by the player.) The data items of interest which were displayed are denoted by "G" in Table 3.7, and include demand, closing inventory, sales, industry sales, demand for a substitute product, GNP, GNP forecast, a production index and a production index forecast for the product using the material the player's company manufactured.

SUMMARY

In this chapter we have discussed the specific operational variables in six studies which will be used to provide empirical support for the descriptive model. This research represents four years of effort and has involved well over 2000 users of information systems in field and laboratory settings.

Not all of the studies furnished data on all parts of the model; certain studies provided evidence only on particular propositions. Certainly, we would prefer to have each study test all propositions in the model. However, a number of new variables were added as the model and research evolved over time. Also, in certain situations the nature of the study made it impossible to include all variables. For example, in the fourth study, the sales force has almost no contact with the information services department, and it would not have been meaningful to measure the sales representatives' attitudes toward the information services department staff.

CAUSALITY

The descriptive model presented in Chapter 2 suggests a number of causal relationships such as "variable A causes, or leads to, variable B." It is very difficult in cross-sectional field research (all data gathered at one point in time) to demonstrate causality.* A positive correlation among variables shows an association; A may cause B, B may cause A, or A and B may be related because some variable C influences both of them. Experimental designs offer more evidence of causality than cross-sectional studies because of better control over confounding variables; however, realistic experiments on information systems are hard to design and execute.

Causal arguments based on cross-sectional data are strengthened if one can reason *a priori* that A had to precede B in time. For example, if an association is noted between having a college degree and salary, it is unlikely that a higher salary caused the acquisition of a degree. However, there may be some other variable not specified in the model which is responsible for the association; possibly higher ambition leads to the completion of college and higher salaries. Another possibility is the existence of an intervening variable, for example, a college degree leads to more confidence which results in a higher salary.

It is likely that for many attitudinal variables there are cycles of mutual

---

* Techniques such as path analysis can be used to strengthen causal arguments from cross-sectional data, but this approach still does not completely solve the causal inference problem. Path analysis is not really suitable for the entire model presented here because of the large number of variables and the fact that different studies apply to different propositions.

causality; for example, A causes B and this feeds back to increase A. Management support may result in more favorable user attitudes and more involvement to result in better systems and ultimately in more management support. For the most part, in testing the propositions we shall only be able to say whether or not the data support the model. However, this limitation is typical of disciplines which involve empirical research.

CHAPTER

FOUR

user attitudes and perceptions

INTRODUCTION

THIS CHAPTER DISCUSSES propositions relating to information services, department policies, and user attitudes and perceptions of the information services staff and systems. For readers unfamiliar with some of the statistical tests presented in this and the next two chapters, at the end of the book there is an Appendix on the different statistical techniques used to analyze the data.*

PROPOSITION 1. SYSTEMS QUALITY

Background

Proposition 1 states that systems design and operations policies of the information services department influence the technical quality of information systems. In this proposition we mean absolute quality, whereas in other propositions quality as perceived by users is the variable of interest. It is difficult to rate the quality of a system because there are no accepted standards. In the University study a panel of information services department staff members contributed ratings for this purpose. However, to test Proposition 1, we need to study the policies of the information ser-

* The more casual reader who is not interested in the details of the evidence may want merely to refer to the summary tables at the end of this and the next two chapters.

vices staff and evaluate the quality of the systems resulting from these policies on some standard.

Because the studies in the preceding chapter do not contain variables explicitly relating information services staff policies to an independent evaluation of systems quality, we have to rely on less systematic case studies to test Proposition 1.

Evidence

One important system, developed by Professor Michael Scott Morton, is an example of what he has classified as "management decision systems" (Scott Morton, 1971). The CRT-based system Scott Morton designed was undertaken as a research project; it was used extensively and is widely considered to be an example of a successful system. The design team observed the decisionmaking sessions of the intended user group and developed a descriptive model of their decision process. This model was used to guide the development of a computerized decision support system and the system was adjusted to the reactions of users. The design team carefully considered the user's decision requirements and the need for a technical design which would facilitate high levels of use. The systems design policy of carefully studying decision requirements and the operations policy of making continual modifications to the implemented system resulted in a successful system with high technical quality.

Another example of a high quality system resulted from an extensive effort which considered user needs and produced a simple, effective system for the United Farm Workers Organizing Committee. The design team felt that it was important to develop a simple system for two major reasons. First, the Union's manual processing methods were in danger of collapse and quick relief was needed; a simple system could be implemented more rapidly. Second, the Union had little experience with computers and a simple system had the greatest chance of being designed and programmed correctly. The result of this policy to develop and operate a technologically simple system combined with careful attention to organizational behavior variables was a highly successful system (Lucas and Plimpton, 1972; Lucas, 1974c). The system has been received enthusiastically and is used extensively.

At the opposite extreme from the two examples cited are cases where the activities of the information services department have been associated with low quality systems. In one instance, design was delegated to an outside consultant and the system was forced on users with no testing or training. (See the Hollister case in Dearden, McFarland, and Zani, 1971.) A thick manual of instructions for entering a large number of different transactions on a terminal was provided, even though many of the workers were illiterate. The system failed and had to be withdrawn. The second attempt to develop a similar system was under the full control of the information services department. The new version was card-oriented and an experiment was conducted to demonstrate that it would work before full scale implementation. Unfortunately, the experiment was overcontrolled by the information services department staff, thus producing misleading results, and this system failed also when it was implemented. Both systems had low quality; they did not work when implemented, and both failures can easily be attributed to the information services department staff activities.

In another case a proposed sales system by the manager of the information services department was clearly of such poor quality that it could not possibly succeed. The design failed to consider input requirements based on a document that salesmen had already refused to submit. (See the Gem Frocks case in Dearden, McFarland, and Zani, 1971.)

In our final case the information services staff used poor procedures to decide on new computer applications. The information services department refused a proposed application which had a very high benefit/cost ratio. From the data presented in the case it is clear that the system had the potential for making a significant contribution to the organization, and the activities of the information services department staff may have prevented the development of a high quality system. (See the Harmony-Life case in Dearden, McFarland, and Zani, 1971.)

In these examples, information services staff activities appear to be directly related to the quality of the resulting system. Though we lack systematic data to support Proposition 1, the evidence from these cases provides support for the proposition that information services department design and operations policies and the execution of the policies influence the quality of information systems.

PROPOSITION 2. SYSTEMS QUALITY AND
USER REACTIONS

Background
In addition to affecting actual systems quality, the approach of the
information services department staff to systems design and operations
should influence user attitudes toward the staff and user perceptions of
systems. The information services department is a service organization
and its policies should influence its customers, that is, users. Data to support Proposition 2 come from the Bay Area study (Lucas, 1973c) and an
empirical study by Dickson and Powers (1973). Dickson and Powers
studied completed projects in depth in a sample of firms in the Min-
neapolis–St. Paul area to determine the correlates of project success. A
diverse range of companies was involved and the researchers included
user satisfaction as a measure of success.*

Evidence
Table 4.1 shows the results relating to Proposition 2 from the Bay
Area study. The information services department operations and design
policies obtained from interviews with the managers of the department
are binary in nature; either they are followed or they are not. For the analysis, users are divided into two groups according to whether their organization's information services department adheres to a particular policy or
not. For example, in Table 4.1 the mean responses on attitudinal and perceptual variables of all respondents where information services department managers report to a vice president or above are compared with the
means for respondents in organizations where the information services
department manager reports below the vice presidential level. (Only statistically significant results are reported in Table 4.1.) The table shows
strong support for the proposition that information services department
operations and design policies are associated with user attitudes and perceptions. What is the nature of the association among these variables?

First, it appears that the reporting level of the information services
department is not too important as evidenced by the mixed results in the

* In the Dickson and Powers paper the direction of associations among variables
is presented, but not the actual numerical results.

Table 4.1. Differences in Mean Responses in the Bay Area Study

	Attitudes and Perceptions [a]				
	A_{22} Attitudes Toward ISD [b] Staff	V_{21} Perceived Input Quality	V_{22} Perceived Output Quality	V_{24} Involvement Reported	V_{25} Training Received
	Means	Means	Means	Means	Means
Operations					
O_{21} Report to					
VP	4.34 [e]	—	4.51 [e]	2.67 [d]	2.95 [d]
Other	4.72	—	4.88	2.37	2.74
O_{22} Steering committee					
Yes	4.28 [e]	—	4.45 [e]	2.67 [c]	—
No	4.66	—	4.82	2.47	—
O_{23} Charge					
Overhead	4.57 [c]	—	4.80 [e]	—	2.79 [c]
User	4.38	—	4.48	—	2.97
O_{24} User Representative					
Yes	—	—	—	2.83 [e]	3.03 [e]
No	—	—	—	2.40	2.77
Systems design					
C_{21} Source of systems					
User	4.58 [c]	4.65 [e]	—	—	2.80 [c]
ISD	4.38	4.98	—	—	2.96
C_{22} Source of changes					
User	4.24 [e]	—	4.32 [e]	—	—
ISD	4.63	—	4.83	—	—
C_{23} File Management packages					
Yes	—	—	—	2.39 [e]	2.77 [e]
No	—	—	—	2.82	3.03
C_{24} On-line systems					
Yes	—	5.00 [e]	4.91 [e]	—	—
No	—	4.70	4.51	—	—

[a] Involvement and training are measured on a 5-point scale and all other variables are measured on a 7-point scale.
[b] Information services department.
[c] $p \leqslant .05$.
[d] $p \leqslant .01$.
[e] $p \leqslant .001$.

table. Reporting to the vice presidential level or above is associated with less favorable user ratings of computer potential and output quality and greater levels of involvement and training. The lack of importance of the reporting position is not surprising because, according to Proposition 6, it is management support that is important, not lines on an organizational chart.

In the Six-Company study described in the preceding chapter, members of a management steering committee in one firm had significantly more favorable attitudes toward information services department staff members than other users. In the Bay Area study all individuals in companies having steering committees were compared with those in companies not using this mechanism. In the Bay Area study steering committee companies reported greater involvement, but attitudes and output quality were less favorably rated than in companies without steering committees. In Table 4.1 the results are for all users in the companies, and the research may not adequately portray the possible benefits of a steering committee. A steering committee may have been formed because of unfavorable attitudes, and some time must elapse before the committee is able to affect user reactions. Instead of this cross-sectional research, a longitudinal study is necessary to evaluate a steering committee: attitudes of both members and nonmembers of the steering committee should be monitored over time.

There has been a trend toward charging users for information services instead of charging all computer expenses to overhead. According to Table 4.1, more favorable attitudes are associated with charging to overhead. We also found that a larger number of reports is associated with charging users for services. This finding suggests that the price mechanism may not work adequately for systems design if users do not understand computer technology well and request unnecessary reports which the staff provides because the user is paying for them. One solution to this problem may be to charge overhead for systems design activities which are highly uncertain and are more of a research and development nature and to charge users for operations where it is easier to determine equitable and predictable charges.

User representatives have been suggested as one approach to integrating the information services department staff with users. The results in Table 4.1 are generally positive for this operational policy; greater involvement and training are reported in companies using these liaison agents.

In Table 4.1 we can see that user attitudes are more favorable in companies where users are generally the source of systems, though, somewhat surprisingly, input quality is rated lower under these conditions. The Dickson and Powers (1973) study also found that user-originated systems were associated with greater user satisfaction, which can be considered a type of attitude. If attitudes are more favorable when users are the source of systems, will the reaction be the same when users are the source of changes? Table 4.1 shows that the answer to this question is negative; it appears that the attitudes and perceptions are more favorable when the information services department staff is the primary source of changes. Such a systems design policy probably indicates a continuing interest in providing better service to the user; the information services department staff makes changes before the user has to request them.

The use of file management packages has been recommended because it allows the user to custom-tailor reports to meet his needs. Under these conditions we expect a greater need for training and more user involvement in computer activities. However, it is interesting to note that, according to Table 4.1, involvement and training appear to be lower in companies using file management packages. (One information services department manager using such a package admitted that he had never spent any funds to train users!)

On-line systems have usually been developed because of their fast response and the ability to update a centralized data base from decentralized geographic locations. On-line systems also represent one way to reduce the voluminous output and improve data collection procedures associated with computer systems. The results in Table 4.1 suggest the benefits of on-line processing; users in companies with on-line systems have more favorable perceptions of input and output quality.

The final variable involved in systems design and operations policies is shown in Table 4.2. The number of reports produced by three major systems in six of the seven companies in the Bay Area study was available (Lucas 1974a). The mean number of reports for these systems in each company was correlated with mean attitude ratings for the six companies. The results are strongly negative; that is, less favorable attitudes are associated with larger numbers of reports, as shown in Table 4.2. This find-

Table 4.2. Pearson Correlation among Mean Attitude Ratings and the Mean Number of Reports in Six Companies

	C_{25} Mean Number of Reports
V_{22} Mean perceived output quality	$-.69$ [a]
A_{22} Mean attitudes toward ISD staff	$-.70$ [a]

[a] $p \le .06$, $n = 6$.

ing may be indicative of information overload; users need more filtered data, not more data (Ackoff, 1967). A larger number of reports was also associated with charging users for computer services. The information services department may exert more discipline in developing new reports when overhead is charged rather than when the user is paying for a requested report himself.

In summary, Proposition 2 receives strong support from the data of the Bay Area study. However, our variables relating to information services department policies could be expanded in future studies to determine the relationship between other policies and user attitudes and perceptions.

PROPOSITION 3. USER CONTACT

Background
Proposition 3 suggests that, under unfavorable conditions, contact with information services staff members will be associated with less favorable attitudes and perceptions on the part of users, and under favorable conditions the opposite relationship will be found. Under adverse conditions it is difficult to form favorable attitudes, particularly when the user is frustrated by what he perceives to be a failure of the information service department.

Evidence
Evidence from the Six-Company study supports this proposition. The correlation among attitudes and contact was not significant, but in a regression analysis the coefficient of contact in predicting attitudes was negative and statistically significant.

Table 4.3. Regression Analysis Predicting User Reactions from the University Study [a]

(4.1) A_{31} *Computer potential* =			(4.2) A_{32} *Attitudes toward ISD staff* =		
+ 1.59			− 1.05		
+ .19 R_{32}	ISD output quality rating	(1.80) [b]	+ .42 R_{31}	ISD input quality rating	(1.68)
+ .05 S_{31}	Position	(1.68)	+ .21 R_{33}	ISD overall quality rating	(1.38)
+ .24 V_{34}	Training	(1.96)	+ .31 V_{32}	Output quality	(2.97)
+ .40 V_{35}	Contact with ISD	(2.32)	+ .18 V_{36}	Management support	(.18)
+ .12 V_{36}	Management support	(1.29)			
+ .49 V_{37}	Suitability of number of reports received	(1.99)			

Equation	n	R	R^2	F	$p \leq$
4.1	80	.51	.26	4.34	.001
4.2	77	.54	.29	7.47	.001

[a] To predict user attitudes, the variables in the ISD ratings, situational, personal, and user perceptions classes in Table 3.3 were included as potential predictor variables in the stepwise regressions.
[b] Numbers in parentheses are t statistics.

Further evidence on the proposition comes from the study of University computing. University users can be divided into two groups: those who use batch computer systems exclusively and those who also work with an on-line system. Examining the results within the exclusive batch group first, Equation 4.1 in Table 4.3 has a positive coefficient for contact (V_{35}) in predicting user attitudes. Within the exclusive batch user group higher levels of contact are associated with more favorable attitudes in this equation, as predicted.

A comparison between the batch and on-line user groups demonstrates that contact under unfavorable circumstances can be associated with less favorable user perceptions. Open-ended comments and observations indicated major implementation problems with the on-line system. A number of users had no choice but to work with the on-line system to process data and retrieve information. Contact with computer activities was significantly higher for the on-line user group when compared with the exclusive batch users group, probably because of the continuing implementation effort. At the same time on-line user ratings of input/output quality were significantly lower than for the batch user group. In this intergroup comparison higher contact under unfavorable circumstances was associated with less favorable user perceptions.

PROPOSITION 4. USER INVOLVEMENT

Background
Proposition 4 suggests that user involvement and participation in systems design and operations are associated with favorable attitudes toward information systems and the information services department staff.

Evidence
The data from the Six-Company and Bay Area studies are shown in Table 4.4; involvement is positively correlated with user ratings of computer potential, but not with attitudes toward the information services department staff. Possibly, involvement in the design of new systems raises expectations as demonstrated by higher ratings of potential, but also creates some dissatisfaction with the staff owing to the limitations of existing systems.

The Dickson and Powers study (1973) also reported that the participation of operating management in design, their approval of specifications, and continued project review were associated with high levels of user satisfaction. The proposition is supported by the data, but more research is needed, particularly longitudinal studies with control groups to see how involvement affects attitudes toward the information services staff.

PROPOSITION 5. SYSTEMS QUALITY AND USER REACTIONS

Background
Proposition 5 suggests that more favorable user attitudes and perception should be associated with systems with higher technical quality. The

Table 4.4. Pearson Correlation Results for Propositions 4–6

	Attitudes toward ISD Staff		Computer Potential	
	$A_{12}{}^a$	$A_{22}{}^b$	$A_{11}{}^a$	$A_{21}{}^b$
Perceived involvement				
V_{13}	NS^e	—	$.22^d$	—
V_{24}	—	NS	—	$.15^d$
Perceived quality of service				
V_{11}	$.40^d$	—	$.50^d$	
V_{21} (input)	—	$.27^d$	—	$.16^d$
V_{22} (output)	—	$.53^d$	—	$.23^d$
Perceived management support				
V_{12}	$.34^d$	—	$.29^c$	—
V_{23}	—	$.29^d$	—	$.07^c$

[a] $n = 683$.
[b] $n = 616$.
[c] $p \leq .05$.
[d] $p \leq .001$.
[e] Not significant.

information services department provides a service to users, and many of the exchanges among its staff and users are focused on the question of service quality.

Evidence
Table 4.4 shows the results from the Six-Company and Bay Area studies. We can see that the perceived quality of service and quality of input/output are highly correlated with favorable attitudes toward the information services department staff and ratings of computer potential. Further evidence to support this proposition is provided in Table 4.3, which predicts attitudes in the University study. Both user perceptions of service quality (training, suitability of the number of reports received) and independent information services department ratings of output quality are positively associated with ratings of computer potential in Equation 4.1. User perceptions of output quality and independent information services department ratings of input quality and overall quality are positively associated with user attitudes toward the information services department

staff in Equation 4.2. On the basis of these data we can conclude that favorable user attitudes and perceptions are strongly associated with the technical quality of systems.

PROPOSITION 6. MANAGEMENT SUPPORT

Background
From Proposition 6 we predict that high levels of management support for and participation in information systems activities should be associated with favorable information services department staff and user attitudes. (The research results only provide data on perceived management actions; there are no variables which explicitly measure managerial behavior.)

Evidence
Data were collected from the information services staff in two studies; 163 staff members in the Six-Company study and 257 staff members in the Bay Area study completed modified user questionnaires. In the Six-Company study the quality of service was correlated .21 with perceived management support,* and in the Bay Area study the rating of input quality was correlated .27 with perceived management support.† Though there are only two significant results, the findings are in the direction predicted by the proposition. There is evidence that perceived management support is positively associated with the attitudes and perceptions of the information services department staff.

Given these results for the information services department staff, are there comparable findings for users? Table 4.4 shows significant correlations between perceived management support and user attitudes in the Six-Company and Bay Area studies. All the results are positive, as expected, but the association is stronger in the Six-Company study. Referring again to the results of Table 4.3 for the University study, we can see that perceived management support (variable V_{36}) is positively associated with user ratings of computer potential and attitudes toward the information services department staff in both equations. Thus Proposition 6 as it applies to users is also supported by the data.

* Pearson correlation, $p < .01$.
† Pearson correlation, $p < .001$.

SUMMARY

In this chapter we have examined the first six propositions of the model; see Table 4.5. The data provided some support for the contention

Table 4.5. Summary of Propositions and Results for Chapter 4

Proposition	Support by Data [a,b]	Studies
1. The systems design and operations policies of the information services department and the execution of these policies influence the technical quality of information systems.	Some support	Individual cases
2. The systems design and operations policies of the information services department influence user attitudes and perceptions of information systems and the information services staff.	Reasonable support	Bay Area study
3. User contact with information services staff members under adverse conditions leads to unfavorable user attitudes and perceptions of information systems and the information services staff.	Weak support	Six-Company study University study
4. User involvement in the design and the operation of information systems results in favorable user attitudes and perceptions of information systems and the information services staff.	Some support	Six-Company study Bay Area study University study
5. Systems with higher technical quality result in more favorable user attitudes and perceptions of information systems and the information services staff.	Strong support	Six-Company study Bay Area study University study
6. High levels of management support for and participation in information systems activities result in favorable information services staff attitudes toward their jobs and users and favorable user attitudes and perceptions of information systems and the information services staff.	Reasonable support	Six-Company study Bay Area study University study

[a] Scored as a continuum 1 2 3 4 5 6 7. (1. Rejected. 2. No evidence. 3. Weak support. 4. Some support. 5. Reasonable support. 6. Strong support. 7. Demonstrated beyond reasonable doubt.)

[b] In developing the rating, factors such as the number of studies, independence of data sources, interstudy consistency, research design, and strength of the findings were considered.

in Proposition 1 that the systems design and operations policies of the information services department influence the quality of information systems. Reasonable support was also provided for Proposition 2; that is, information services department design and operations policies are associated with user attitudes. Proposition 3 concerning user contact with the information services staff received only weak support from the studies.

User involvement in the design and operation of information systems is positively associated with computer potential, but not attitudes toward the information services staff, furnishing some support for Proposition 4. We found strong support in three studies for Proposition 5, which argues that high quality systems are associated with favorable user attitudes and perceptions of information systems and the information systems staff. Finally, the data provided positive evidence on Proposition 6 relating to management support, though we were only able to measure perceived management support, not actual management actions.

Two findings from this chapter are of major importance. First, the various user-oriented policies of the information systems department for systems design and operations are associated with favorable user attitudes and perceptions of systems. Second, the technical quality of systems is also positively related to favorable user attitudes and perceptions of information systems. These two relationships are important because user attitudes and perceptions must be favorable if information systems are to succeed.

CHAPTER
FIVE

the use of information systems

INTRODUCTION

 IN THIS CHAPTER we discuss propositions which relate to the use of information systems by a decisionmaker. If a system is not used, it cannot be considered a success no matter what its technical elegance and sophistication.

PROPOSITION 7. FAVORABLE USER ATTITUDES

Background

This proposition suggests that favorable user attitudes and perceptions of information systems and the information services department lead to high levels of use of information systems. We should really qualify this proposition to distinguish between voluntary and involuntary use. Supplying input to a system is often involuntary and the output of some systems must be used, for example, a payroll or billing system. However, different levels of use are possible for much of the information provided by information systems beyond the strictly transactions processing systems discussed in Chapter 1. For instance, one sales representative may only glance at a sales report while another one may analyze it in detail.

According to Proposition 7, high levels of voluntary use of a system are consistent with favorable attitudes. Much of the use of the systems in the studies discussed here is voluntary in nature and, in general, we should expect to find favorable attitudes associated with high levels of system use. However, in the case of a system which is used involuntarily, we may find higher levels of use associated with unfavorable attitudes developed because of the mandatory use of a low quality system.

Evidence

Table 5.1 presents the results of a regression analysis predicting the use of information systems in the University study. Equations 5.1 and 5.2 reflect usage of 26 University batch systems; it is expected that the use of these systems is highly voluntary since most of the systems produce a variety of output reports. The amount of time spent and the extent of the analysis of the reports is generally at the discretion of the user.

Equations 5.1 and 5.2 demonstrate that user perceptions and attitudes are positively associated with high levels of system use. Ratings of computer potential and the suitability of the number of reports received all have positive coefficients in these two equations. The negative coefficient for the desire for more summary and exception reports in Equation 5.1 may be interpreted as favorable because it signifies that users are satisfied with the present format of reports.

The data from the University study also support the qualification of Proposition 7 that forced use of a low quality system is associated with less favorable user attitudes. The University had been developing an on-line system at the time of the study and only portions of it had been implemented. The system encountered a number of serious problems. Users no longer received their familiar batch reports, and they had to rely on the on-line system, at least for operational control data.

Equations 5.3 and 5.4 in Table 5.1 show the results of the regression analysis of use of the on-line system. Use is positively related to user perceptions of systems quality (V_{33}) and the independent information services department ratings of systems performance, overall quality, and usefulness. The use of the system, however, is negatively related to information services department ratings of output quality, documentation, training, and accuracy. In Equation 5.4 user ratings of computer potential are also positive predictors of use.

In spite of the problems encountered with this system, a number of the attitudinal and perceptional variables are still positive predictors of sys-

Table 5.1. Regression Analysis Predicting the Use of Information from the University Study [a]

(5.1)	(5.2)
U_{31} *Batch system (general use)* =	U_{32} *Batch use (various purposes)* =

$+4.80$
- $-$ .46 R_{31} ISD input quality rating (1.88) [b]
- $+$ .50 R_{35} ISD system usefulness rating (2.78)
- $-$ .18 I_{31} Education (2.51)
- $+$ .21 A_{31} Computer potential (1.82)
- $+$ .45 V_{37} Suitability of number of reports Received (1.78)
- $-$ .20 V_{38} Would like more summary/exception reports (1.56)

$+1.07$
- $+$ .56 R_{33} ISD overall quality rating (2.58)
- $+$ .10 S_{31} Position (2.17)
- $+$ .49 V_{37} Suitability of number of reports received (1.34)

(5.3)	(5.4)
U_{33} *On-line system use (special features)* =	U_{34} *On-line system (general use)* =

$-$ .70
- $+$ 1.25 R_{33} ISD overall quality rating (4.52)
- $-$ 1.70 R_{36} ISD documentation, training, accuracy rating (5.54)
- $+$ 1.24 R_{37} ISD on-line performance rating (2.03)
- $-$ .36 A_{32} Attitudes toward ISD staff (2.37)
- $+$ .88 V_{33} On-line system rating (6.71)

$-$ 5.42
- $-$ 2.40 R_{32} ISD output quality rating (3.99)
- $+$ 1.04 R_{33} ISD overall quality rating (3.20)
- $+$ 1.48 R_{35} ISD system usefulness rating (2.96)
- $+$ 1.80 R_{37} ISD on-line performance rating (2.05)
- $+$ .52 A_{31} Computer potential (2.87)
- $-$ .70 A_{32} Attitudes toward ISD staff (3.68)
- $+$ .85 V_{33} On-line system rating (4.98)

Equation	n	R	R^2	F	$p \leq$
5.1	80	.56	.32	5.65	.001
5.2	79	.43	.19	3.75	.010
5.3	37	.86	.74	17.44	.001
5.4	36	.82	.67	8.06	.001

[a] To predict the use of information, variables in the ISD ratings, situational, personal, user attitudes, and user perceptions classes in Table 3.3 were included as potential predictor variables in the stepwise regressions.
[b] Numbers in parentheses are t statistics.

tems use. However, in both Equations 5.3 and 5.4, attitudes toward the information services department staff are negatively associated with use, supporting the qualification of Proposition 7 that the required use of a problem system may be associated with unfavorable user attitudes.

Data from the Sales Force study also support Proposition 7, as shown in Table 5.2. Of the 17 equations predicting the use of the information system in the three divisions of the company, all contain at least one perceptual or attitudinal variable. A total of 26 attitudinal or perceptual variables appear in the 17 equations, and 23 of the beta weights have positive coefficients as predicted by Proposition 7.* †

Perceptions of information systems were also included in the Branch Bank study, shown in Table 5.3. One of these variables rates the output quality of the information system (V_{51}), and this variable appears in four of the eight equations predicting use in Table 5.3. In each instance the beta weight for output quality is positive as predicted.

PROPOSITION 8. DECISION STYLE

Background

Proposition 8 indicates that differing decision styles should be associated with differing levels of use of information systems and different actions based on information. Unfortunately there is no widely accepted definition of decision style; the field studies included variables which distinguish between users who keep their own records and who perform analyses on data and those who rely completely on the information furnished them. We can classify the groups keeping records and performing calculations as more analytic and information-oriented. Data from the Laboratory Experiment include one variable which distinguishes among decision styles based on a scale of the Myers-Briggs test.

* The negative coefficients are probably due to multicollinearity among the attitudinal variables.
† The beta weight is a standardized measure which is independent of the measurement unit; it represents the change in the dependent variable measured in number of standard deviations resulting from a change of one standard deviation in an independent variable controlling for all other independent variables.

Evidence

The results for the Sales Force study in Table 5.2 show that keeping additional item level records in Equations 5.5, 5.7, and 5.14 is positively associated with the use of the system, while keeping these records is negatively associated with use in Equations 5.12, 5.18, and 5.20. The same type of results can be observed for D_{42}, performing additional calculations on the report. The evidence from this study is mixed as to the direction of the association between decision style and use, but the association itself is significant.

In the Branch Bank study, decision style is also important, as we can see in Table 5.2. Use is generally positively associated with the number of customer calls made during the month by branch bank management personnel. The use of reports from the information system is generally negatively associated with variables D_{53} through D_{55}, which relate to activism and exceeding limits. These variables may characterize the more intuitive and aggressive manager who has less need for formal reports.

In the Laboratory Experiment, decision style was measured using the Sensing-Intuition scale of the Myers-Briggs test which has been recommended by other researchers as an instrument for assessing cognitive style (Mason and Mitroff, 1973). Table 5.4 presents the only usage variables from Table 3.7 which are significantly correlated with decision style. High values on the test score for decision style denote a more intuitive decisionmaker. The few findings seem somewhat surprising, as we might hypothesize that more analytic decisionmakers make greater use of formal reports. Instead, the large proportion of positive correlations indicates that report usage is higher among intuitive individuals. Perhaps analytic decisionmakers have a consistent strategy which they follow in the game, while the intutitive decisionmaker formulates plans for each playing session and needs information for this purpose.

In summary, the results from the three research studies confirm the existence of a relationship between decision style and the use of information. However, further research is necessary to determine how decision style affects information use, particularly research with psychological tests in field settings.

Proposition 8 also suggests that the likelihood of taking action based on information from an information system will vary with differing decision

Table 5.2. Standardized Regressions Predicting the Use of Information Systems from the Sales Force Study [a]

Division A

(5.5)

$U_{41}^{b,c}$ *Working with customer in store* =

−.23 S_{41} Number of accounts   (2.53)[d]

+.16 D_{41}[e]   Keeps own records   (1.79)

+.31 A_{41} Computer potential   (3.46)

(5.6)

U_{42}^c *Detailed analysis of buying entity/account* =

−.38 S_{43} Length of time in territory   (5.02)

−.09 I_{42} Education   (1.24)

+.31 A_{41} Computer potential   (4.01)

+.25 V_{41} Output quality   (3.08)

+.14 V_{42} Management support   (1.90)

(5.7)

U_{43} *Overall progress* =

−.15 P_{41} Total dollar bookings 1972 season   (1.84)

−.27 S_{44} Length of time in position   (2.55)

+.13 I_{41} Age   (1.25)

+.14 D_{41}[e]   Keeps own records   (1.71)

+.18 A_{41} Computer potential   (1.96)

+.38 V_{41} Output quality   (4.24)

(5.8)

U_{44} *Summary this year versus last* =

−.20 S_{42} Number of buying entities   (2.21)

−.25 S_{43} Length of time in territory   (2.77)

+.22 V_{42} Management support   (2.45)

(5.9)

U_{45} *Planning* =

−.25 S_{41} Number of accounts   (3.32)

+.22 S_{43} Length of time in territory   (1.63)

−.45 S_{44} Length of time in position   (3.35)

+.19 D_{42}[e]   Performs calculations on report   (2.62)

+.21 A_{41} Computer potential   (2.66)

+.34 V_{41} Output quality   (4.25)

(5.10)

U_{46} *Cancellations* =

−.19 P_{41} Total dollar bookings 1972 season   (1.94)

−.17 S_{44} Length of time in position   (1.47)

+.20 I_{41} Age   (1.77)

+.24 V_{41} Output quality   (2.48)

+.18 V_{42} Management support   (1.85)

Division B

(5.11)
U_{41}^{c} *Working in store with customer* =

$-.17\ I_{42}$	Education	(1.12)
$+.26\ V_{41}$	Output quality	(1.66)

(5.12)
U_{42}^{c} *Detailed analysis of buying entity/account* =

$+.28\ S_{44}$	Length of time in position	(1.90)
$-.34\ I_{41}$	Age	(2.38)
$-.22\ I_{42}$	Education	(1.57)
$-.21\ D_{41}^{e}$	Keeps own records	(1.53)
$+.43\ A_{41}$	Computer potential	(2.98)

(5.13)
U_{43} *Overall progress* =

$+.18\ S_{42}$	Number of buying entities	(1.27)
$-.22\ I_{42}$	Education	(1.47)
$+.35\ V_{42}$	Management support	(2.31)

(5.14)
U_{44} *Summary this year versus last* =

$+.27\ S_{43}$	Length of time in territory	(1.81)
$-.29\ S_{44}$	Length of time in position	(1.84)
$-.41\ I_{42}$	Education	(2.99)
$+.14\ D_{41}^{e}$	Keeps own records	(1.05)
$+.40\ A_{41}$	Computer potential	(2.89)
$-.11\ V_{41}$	Output quality	(.77)

(5.15)
U_{45} *Planning* =

$-.17\ P_{41}$	Total dollar bookings 1972 season	(1.16)
$+.33\ S_{41}$	Number of accounts	(2.42)
$-.21\ S_{42}$	Number of buying entities	(1.32)
$-.27\ I_{41}$	Age	(1.90)
$-.29\ I_{42}$	Education	(2.14)
$+.37\ V_{41}$	Output quality	(2.88)

(5.16)
U_{46} *Cancellations* =

$+.21\ S_{43}$	Length of time in territory	(1.50)
$-.26\ I_{41}$	Age	(1.86)
$-.21\ I_{42}$	Education	(1.55)
$+.41\ A_{41}$	Computer potential	(2.93)

Table 5.2 continued

Division C

(5.17) $U_{41}{}^c$ Working with customer in store =

Coeff.	Var.	Description	(t)
+.46	S_{41}	Number of accounts	(2.89)
-.26	S_{42}	Number of buying entities	(1.61)
+.25	S_{43}	Length of time in territory	(1.77)
+.45	S_{44}	Length of time in position	(3.36)
-.30	I_{41}	Age	(2.59)
+.59	V_{41}	Output quality	(5.30)

(5.18) $U_{42}{}^c$ Detailed analysis of buying entity/account =

Coeff.	Var.	Description	(t)
-.40	$D_{41}{}^e$	Keeps own records	(2.16)
+.54	V_{41}	Output quality	(3.06)
+.25	V_{42}	Management support	(1.21)

(5.19) U_{44} Summary this year versus last =

Coeff.	Var.	Description	(t)
-.37	S_{44}	Length of time in position	(2.04)
+.41	I_{41}	Age	(2.25)
+.51	V_{42}	Management support	(3.11)

(5.20) U_{45} Planning =

Coeff.	Var.	Description	(t)
-.21	P_{41}	Total dollar bookings 1972 season	(1.26)
-.05	S_{41}	Number of accounts	(.17)
+.39	S_{42}	Number of buying entities	(1.25)
-.55	I_{42}	Education	(2.84)
-.23	$D_{41}{}^e$	Keeps own records	(1.43)
-.46	$D_{42}{}^e$	Performs calculations on report	(2.43)
+.74	A_{41}	Computer potential	(4.16)
-.28	V_{41}	Output quality	(1.52)

(5.21) U_{46} Cancellations =

Coeff.	Var.	Description	(t)
+.16	S_{41}	Number of accounts	(.81)
+.46	S_{43}	Length of time in territory	(2.07)
-.30	I_{41}	Age	(1.32)
+.30	$D_{42}{}^e$	Performs calculations on report	(1.61)
-.32	$A_{41}{}^e$	Computer potential	(1.41)
+.49	V_{42}	Management support	(2.37)

Equation	n	R	R^2	F	$P <$	$R_v^{2\,f}$
5.5	104	.46	.21	8.76	.001	.03
5.6	104	.72	.52	21.33	.001	.03
5.7	104	.62	.38	10.10	.001	.09
5.8	104	.41	.17	6.89	.001	.03
5.9	104	.71	.51	17.28	.001	.10
5.10	104	.45	.20	4.87	.001	.04
5.11	43	.36	.13	3.02	NS [g]	
5.12	43	.57	.32	3.58	.010	
5.13	43	.40	.16	2.62	NS	
5.14	43	.65	.42	4.49	.010	
5.15	43	.66	.43	4.63	.010	
5.16	43	.52	.27	3.64	.001	
5.17	24	.90[h]	.81[h]	14.66	.001	
5.18	24	.66[h]	.43[h]	7.03	.010	
5.19	24	.60[h]	.36[h]	5.41	.010	
5.20	24	.70[h]	.49[h]	4.11	.010	
5.21	24	.48[h]	.23[h]	2.23	NS	

[a] To predict the use of information, variables in the situational, personal, decision style, user attitudes, and user perceptions classes in Table 3.4 were included as potential predictor variables in the stepwise regressions. In addition, performance was included as a potential predictor for variables U_{43} through U_{46}, the usage scales classified as problem finding in nature.

[b] Because of the wide range of values, standardized beta weights are presented rather than the actual regression coefficients. The beta weight represents the change in the dependent variable in number of standard deviations resulting from a standardized unit increase in an independent variable with all other independent variables held constant.

[c] Variables used to predict performance; performance not included as a predictor of use.

[d] Numbers in parentheses are t statistics.

[e] Dummy (0, 1) variable; only the sign, not the magnitude of the beta weight is meaningful.

[f] R^2 for validation sample; originally the sample for Division A was divided into a 60% sample for analysis ($n = 104$) and a 40% sample of validation ($n = 71$). R_v^2 is the squared correlation of the actual values from the validation sample and the values predicted for the validation sample using the coefficients of regression equations (5.5–5.16).

[g] NS = not significant.   [h] Adjusted R, R^2.

Table 5.3. Standardized Regressions Predicting the Use of Information Systems from the Branch Bank Study [a]

(5.22)
U'_{51} [b,c,d] *Branch objectives* =

−.19 S_{55} [f]	Transitional customer base	(2.54) [e]
−.12 I_{51}	Age	(1.56)
−.16 I_{55}	Education	(2.11)
+.17 D_{52}	Number of customer calls	(2.32)
−.21 D_{55}	Needs approvals	(2.85)
+.20 V_{51}	Output quality	(2.73)
+.20 V_{52}	Involvement in setting goals	(2.75)

(5.23)
U'_{51} *Branch objectives* =

+.43 V'_{52}	Involvement in setting goals	(4.01)
+.19 V'_{53}	Compensation based on goals	(5.27)

(5.24)
U_{52} *Monthly profit summary* =

+.24 D_{52}	Number of customer calls	(3.30)
+.25 V_{51}	Output quality	(3.42)
+.28 V_{52}	Involvement in setting goals	(3.83)

(5.25)
U'_{52} *Monthly profit summary* =

−.11 S_{54} [f]	Stable customer base	(1.47)
+.23 I_{51}	Age	(2.74)
−.15 I_{54}	Years at branch	(1.78)
+.34 V'_{52}	Involvement in setting goals	(4.42)

(5.26)
U_{53} *Monthly deposit, loan balance, income/expense report* =

+.11 D_{53}	Activism	(1.37)
+.13 V_{51}	Output quality	(1.68)

(5.27)
U_{53} *Monthly deposit, loan balance, income/expense report* =

−.11 S_{51} [f]	High potential location	(1.50)
−.11 S_{58} [f]	Light competition	(1.50)
−.17 I_{54}	Years at branch	(2.25)
−.17 D_{55}	Needs approvals	(2.23)
+.38 V'_{52}	Involvement in setting goals	(5.16)

(5.28) U_{54} Daily statement =

$+.21\ S_{55}^{f}$ Transitional customer base (2.78)
$+.16\ S_{57}^{f}$ Heavy competition (2.08)
$-.16\ I_{55}$ Education (2.07)
$+.16\ D_{52}$ Number of customer calls (2.08)
$-.13\ D_{54}$ Makes exceptions (1.63)
$+.18\ V_{52}$ Involvement in setting goals (2.32)

(5.29) U'_{54} Daily statement =

$-.22\ P_{51}$ Weighted actual performance 1972 (2.82)
$+.11\ S_{55}^{f}$ Transitional customer base (1.46)
$-.12\ I_{52}$ Years at bank (1.44)
$-.14\ I_{55}$ Education (1.72)
$+.12\ D_{51}^{f}$ Keeps own records (1.50)
$-.16\ D_{53}$ Activism (1.98)
$+.15\ V'_{51}$ Output quality (1.84)
$+.19\ V'_{52}$ Involvement in setting goals (2.17)
$+.16\ V'_{53}$ Compensation based on goals (1.88)

Equation	n	R	R^2	F	$p \leq$
5.22	154	.48	.23	6.30	.001
5.23	128	.45	.20	15.48	.001
5.24	154	.46	.21	13.53	.001
5.25	146	.43	.19	8.14	.001
5.26	154	.21	.04	2.19	NS [g]
5.27	146	.51	.26	9.79	.001
5.28	154	.40	.16	4.65	.001
5.29	146	.48	.23	4.58	.001

[a] To predict the use of information, variables in the performance (P_{51} only), situational, personal, decision style, and user perception classes in table 3.5 were included as potential predictor variables in the stepwise regression. The reports included are those for which the likelihood of taking action based on the information in the report is associated with performance. See Tables 6.2 and 6.3.

[b] Because of the wide range of values, standardized beta weights are presented rather than the actual regression coefficients. The beta weight represents the change in the dependent variable in number of standard deviations resulting from a standardized unit increase in an independent variable with all other independent variables held constant.

[c] Prime denotes assistant manager; all other variables are for managers.

[d] Only the usage equations are reported for which action taken on the basis of the report was associated with performance. See Chapter 6.

[e] Numbers in parentheses are t statistics.

[f] Dummy (0, 1) variable; only the sign, not the magnitude, of the beta weight is meaningful.

[g] Not significant.

Table 5.4. Pearson Correlation among Report Usage and Decision Style in the Experiment (D_{61}) [a]

	Current Status of Shipments		
IE		*Exec*	
U_{61}^C General use	$.22^c$ (36) [b]	U_{62}^C Blocked space/ leased warehouse	$.32$ [d] (43)
U_{62}^C Blocked space/ leased warehouse	$.24^c$ (36)		

	Inventory Position		
MBA		*Exec*	
U_{62}^I Select carrier	$-.25$ [c] (36)	U_{66}^I Locate inventory problems	$.29$ [d] (43)

	Profit and Loss				
MBA		*IE*		*Exec*	
U_{61}^P General use	$-.38$ [d] (36)	U_{64}^P Blocked space/ leased warehouse	$.33$ [d] (36)	U_{61}^P General use	$.29$ [d] (43)
				U_{62}^P Uncontrollable costs	$.29$ [d] (43)
				U_{63}^P Controllable costs	$.23$ [c] (43)

	Statistical and Economic Indicators	
	Exec [e]	
	U_{61}^S Value	$.37$ [d] (28)
	U_{62}^S Problem finding	$.35$ [d] (28)

[a] High values of D_{61} are associated with intuitive decisionmaking, low values with a sensing or analytical decision style.
[b] The number of players is listed in parentheses.
[c] $P \leq .10$.
[d] $P \leq .05$.
[e] A subgroup of two treatments using CRT.

styles. (The data make it possible only to measure the likelihood of taking action, not whether action is actually taken.) Data from the Branch Bank study support this contention, as shown in Table 5.5. In general, managers who keep their own records are associated with a greater likelihood of taking action, suggesting that possibly the information system is insufficient as a basis for action and that supplemental records are needed. Other than this observation, a variety of decision style variables are significantly associated with the likelihood of taking action, but the signs of the beta weights vary in Equations 5.30 through 5.37 (Table 5.5), making it difficult to generalize about the direction of the relationship.

PROPOSITION 9. PERSONAL AND SITUATIONAL FACTORS

Background

From Proposition 9 we predict that different personal and situational factors lead to differing levels of use of an information system and action. In general, it is difficult to predict the impact of personal and situational factors because of the unique environment of each organization and the unique position of each individual in the organization.

Evidence

Situational and personal variables are associated with the use of an information system in the University study. In Table 5.1, position is positively associated with, and education negatively related to, the use of batch systems.

In the Sales Force study a variety of personal and situational factors are significantly associated with system use; however, the direction of the association is not consistent, as shown in Table 5.2. In some instances, having a large number of accounts predicts high levels of use and vice versa. Generally, less time in the sales position is associated with high levels of use; possibly newer sales representatives use the system to learn about their clients and territory. The use of the system to work in the store with customers is associated with a longer time in position in Division C (Table 5.2), suggesting that learning and familiarity with the sales report are necessary before it is used in the store with the customer.

Table 5.5 Standardized Regressions Predicting the Likelihood of Taking Action from the Branch Bank Study [a]

(5.30) E_{51} [b,c,d] *Monthly profit summary (call attention)* =

+.17 S_{56}[e]	Hub office competition	(2.25)[f]
+.10 I_{51}	Age	(1.30)
+.34 U_{52}	Monthly profit summary	(3.55)
+.13 D_{51}[e]	Keeps own records	(1.75)
−.13 D_{52}	Number of customer calls	(1.71)
−.14 D_{54}	Makes exceptions	(1.94)
+.21 D_{59}[e]	Studies report in detail	(2.22)
−.13 V_{51}	Output quality	(1.72)
+.14 V_{53}	Compensation based on goals	(1.74)

(5.31) E_{52} *Monthly deposit, loan balance, income/expense report (call attention)* =

.14 S_{56}[e]	Hub office competition	(1.76)
+.27 I_{51}	Age	(2.51)
−.21 I_{52}	Years at bank	(1.91)
+.24 U_{53}	Monthly deposit, loan balance income/expense report	(2.97)
−.11 D_{54}	Makes exceptions	(1.40)
+.15 D_{57}[e]	Looks for exceptions	(1.87)

(5.32) E_{53} *Daily statement (call attention)* =

−.13 S_{58}[e]	Light competition	(1.74)
+.26 U_{54}	Daily statement	(3.23)
+.15 D_{54}	Makes exceptions	(1.92)
−.11 D_{56}[e]	Scans report	(1.41)
−.13 V_{51}	Output quality	(1.59)
+.15 V_{53}	Compensation based on goals	(1.93)

(5.33) E'_{53} *Daily statement (call attention)* =

−.15 S_{52}[e]	Static location	(1.88)
+.25 S_{56}[e]	Hub office	(3.11)
−.20 I_{54}	Years at branch	(2.49)
+.15 I_{55}	Education	(1.94)
+.31 U'_{54}	Daily statement	(4.03)
+.15 D'_{52}	Number of customer calls	(1.98)
+.11 D'_{53}	Activism	(1.38)
−.22 D'_{57}[e]	Looks for exceptions	(2.80)
−.15 D'_{58}[e]	Reads summary information	(1.94)

(5.34) E_{54} *Branch objectives (reallocate efforts)* =

+.15 S_{52}[e]	Static location	(2.04)
+.32 U_{51}	Branch objectives	(3.91)
+.16 D_{51}[e]	Keeps own records	(2.16)
+.11 D_{54}	Makes exceptions	(1.56)
−.18 D_{55}	Needs approvals	(2.28)
−.26 D_{56}[e]	Scans report	(3.30)
−.14 V_{51}	Output quality	(1.81)
+.16 V_{53}	Compensation based on goals	(2.05)

(5.35) E_{54} *Branch objectives (reallocate efforts)* =

−.13 S_{52}[e]	Static location	(1.84)
+.21 S_{54}[e]	Stable customer base	(2.85)
+.29 I_{51}	Age	(3.98)
+.47 U'_{51}	Branch objectives	(6.40)
−.17 D'_{58}[e]	Reads summary information	(2.32)

(5.36)
E_{55} Monthly profit summary (reallocate efforts) =

(5.37)
E_{56} Monthly deposit, loan balance, income/expense report (reallocate efforts) =

Equation	n	R	R^2	F	$p \leq$
5.30	141	.57	.32	6.88	.001
5.31	141	.39	.16	4.10	.001
5.32	152	.41	.17	4.96	.001
5.33	134	.56	.32	6.46	.001
5.34	141	.57	.33	8.14	.001
5.35	134	.58	.34	12.97	.001
5.36	141	.60	.36	9.39	.001
5.37	141	.44	.19	8.01	.001

Equation (5.36):

$+.13\ S_{52}^{e}$ Static location (1.69)

$+.33\ U_{52}$ Monthly profit summary (3.75)

$+.11\ D_{51}^{e}$ Keeps own records (1.50)

$-.11\ D_{55}$ Needs approvals (1.45)

$-.18\ D_{56}^{e}$ Scans report (2.03)

$-.09\ D_{58}^{e}$ Reads summary information (1.31)

$+.13\ V_{52}$ Involvement in setting goals (1.82)

$+.21\ V_{53}$ Compensation based on goals (2.92)

Equation (5.37):

$+.21\ U_{53}$ Monthly deposit, loan balance, income/expense report (2.38)

$+.11\ D_{54}$ Makes exceptions on limits (1.38)

$+.24\ D_{57}^{e}$ Looks for exceptions (3.03)

$+.18\ D_{59}^{e}$ Studies report in detail (2.03)

[a] To predict the likelihood of taking action, variables in the situational, personal, use, decision style, and user perception classes in Table 3.5 were included as potential predictor variables in the stepwise regressions. The actions included are those which are related to performance. See Tables 6.2 and 6.3.

[b] Because of the wide range of values, standardized beta weights are presented rather than the actual regression coefficients. The beta weight represents the change in the dependent variable measured in number of standard deviations resulting from a standardized unit increase in an independent variable with all other independent variables held constant.

[c] Prime denotes assistant managers; all other variables are for managers.

[d] Only the equations as reported for which action was taken on the basis of the report are associated with performance. See Chapter 6.

[e] Dummy (0, 1) variable; only the sign, not the magnitude, of the beta weight is meaningful.

[f] Numbers in parentheses are t statistics.

In Table 5.3 the results predicting use of the information system in the Branch Bank study also demonstrate the importance of personal and situational factors. Again, the direction of the relationship between these factors and use is not consistent, though use does appear to be negatively associated with the educational level of managers and assistant managers.

Data from the Branch Bank also demonstrate the existence of a relationship between personal and situational factors and the likelihood of taking action based on the results in Table 5.5. Being located in a hub location and having a stable customer base is associated with a greater likelihood of taking action. Managers may be placed in these high activity branches because they are judged by their superiors to be more effective or they may actually be forced to take action by the situation. Assistant managers appear less likely to take action in a static location than in other locations, while managers in a static location situation appear to be more likely to take action.

In summary, the evidence supports Proposition 9; situational and personal factors are associated significantly with the use of information systems and the likelihood of taking action. However, making predictions based on these factors is difficult, as we can see by the variety of results within and between studies.

PROPOSITION 10. SYSTEM QUALITY

Background
Proposition 10 contends that the level of use of an information system should be positively related to the technical quality of the system. Where use is voluntary, a highly regarded system should be used more than a poor system.

Evidence
One purpose of the University study was to test explicitly Proposition 10. Systems quality was rated by the information services department staff on user criteria independently from user perceptions on the user questionnaire. In Table 5.1, Equations 5.1 and 5.2 show that higher quality systems as rated by the information services department staff and fa-

vorable user perceptions of service are generally positively associated with the level of systems use.

User ratings of the suitability of the number of reports received and high ratings for the present format of reports (a negative coefficient on variable V_{38}) are related to systems use. Independent information services department ratings of systems usefulness in Equation 5.1 and overall quality in Equation 5.2 are positively related to use. Only the information services department rating of input quality is negatively associated with use and, as noted before, input is one of the least voluntary aspects of use. It is interesting to note that, even for the problem on-line system, high ratings of overall quality by the information services staff are generally positively associated with the level of use of the on-line system. Independent information services department ratings of overall systems quality, systems usefulness, and on-line system performance are positively associated with high levels of use of the on-line system. In Table 5.1, information services department ratings of documentation, training, and accuracy in Equation 5.3 and output quality in Equation 5.4 are the only staff ratings which are negatively associated with the use of the on-line system.

In the Sales Force study, user perceptions of output quality are positively related to the use of the system in eight equations and negatively related in two of the seventeen equations predicting use in Table 5.2. In the Branch Bank study, usage in four equations in Table 5.3 is associated with user perceptions of output quality and all of the relationships are positive. Thus, the three studies provide strong support for Proposition 10. Both user perceptions of system quality and independent ratings of quality are generally positively associated with levels of use of an information system.

PROPOSITION 11. ACTION

Background
Many times a decisionmaker will take action based on the information he receives. He may act to find the cause of, or a solution to, a problem and the action can include working with an employee, a cus-

tomer, a supplier, etc. According to Proposition 11, we expect that high levels of use of an information system increase the probability that a decisionmaker will take action based on the data provided by the system.

Evidence

Table 5.5 contains the results of the regressions predicting the likelihood that branch management personnel will take action based on information in the reports. (The actions included are those associated with performance; see Chapter 6.) In each of the eight equations in Table 5.5, use of the report is significantly and positively associated with the likelihood that the manager or assistant manager will take action. The results do support the proposition, though we have data from only one study and are able to consider only the likelihood of taking action, not whether action was taken.

SUMMARY

In this chapter we have discussed evidence on the propositions from the descriptive model dealing with factors affecting the use of information and the likelihood of taking action. The results are summarized in Table 5.6. Proposition 7 concerning the association between favorable user attitudes and high levels of system use was strongly supported by the data from several studies. Proposition 8 was also supported by the data; decision style appears to be associated with differing levels of use of information systems and the likelihood of taking action based on the information. However, there seems to be little consistency in the direction of the relationships.

The data also agree with the contention that personal and situational factors are associated with the use of systems and the likelihood of taking action, though there is little apparent consistency in the direction of the relationships. Data on user perceptions and independent information services department ratings strongly support Proposition 10, which states that higher quality systems should be associated with higher levels of systems use. Finally, the data from a single study support Proposition 11, which contends that higher levels of use of an information system are associated with a greater likelihood that a decisionmaker will take action based on information.

Table 5.6. Summary of Propositions and Results for Chapter 5

Proposition	Support by data [a,b]	Studies
7. Favorable user attitudes and perceptions of information systems and the information services staff lead to high levels of use of an information system.	Strong support	University study Sales Force study Branch Bank study
8. Individuals with differing decision styles have differing levels of use of information systems, perform different analyses of data, and take different actions based on information.	Reasonable support	University study Branch Bank study Laboratory experiment
9. Different situational and personal factors lead to differing levels of use of an information system and actions.	Reasonable support	University study Sales Force study Branch Bank study
10. High levels of system use result from a system with high technical quality.	Strong support	University study Sales Force study Branch Bank study
11. High levels of use of an information system make it more likely that a user will take action based on the information provided.	Some support	Branch bank study

[a] Scored as a continuum 1 2 3 4 5 6 7. (1. Rejected. 2. No evidence. 3. Weak support. 4. Some support. 5. Reasonable support. 6. Strong support. 7. Demonstrated beyond reasonable doubt.)
[b] In developing the rating, factors such as the number of studies, independence of data sources, interstudy consistency, research design, and strength of the findings were considered.

The two most important findings in this chapter are that favorable user attitudes and perceptions and high technical systems quality are associated with high levels of use of an information system. For a system to be a success, it must be used; understanding the factors associated with high levels of use should help us design successful systems.

CHAPTER
SIX

performance and information systems

INTRODUCTION

IN THIS CHAPTER we complete the presentation of the data from the studies to test the descriptive model of information systems in the context of the organization. The discussion centers around propositions relating to performance because one way to evaluate an information system is on its contribution to performance.

PROPOSITION 12. DECISION STYLE

Background

In Chapter 5 we found support for Proposition 8 which suggested that decision style is associated with use of information and the likelihood of taking action based on information. In this chapter we want to see if the evidence supports the prediction from Proposition 12 that different decision styles are associated with different levels of performance.

Evidence

The results of the regression analysis predicting sales representative performance in the Sales Force study may be found in Table 6.1. In Divison A, keeping item level records is positively associated with performance, while in Division B, performing calculations with the data from the sales report is negatively associated with performance. These

Table 6.1. Standardized Regressions Predicting Sales Representative Performance from the Sales Force Study[a]

Division A (6.1)	Division B (6.2)	Division C (6.3)
P_{41} Total dollar bookings, 1972 season =	P_{41} Total dollar bookings, 1972 season =	P_{41} Total dollar bookings, 1972 season =
−.30 S_{41}[b] Number of accounts (2.31)[c]	+.28 S_{42} Number of buying entities (2.03)	−.24 S_{42} Number of buying entities (1.30)
+.35 S_{42} Number of buying entities (2.64)	+.19 S_{44} Time in position (1.37)	+.39 S_{44} Time in position (2.24)
+.32 S_{44} Time in position (3.51)	+.28 I_{42} Education (2.03)	+.27 U_{41} Working with customer in store (1.41)
+.16 D_{41}[d] Keeps own records (1.78)	−.21 D_{42}[d] Performs calculations on report (1.47)	

Equation	n	R	R^2	F	$p \leq$	R^{2}[e]
(6.1)	104	.44	.19	6.05	.01	.21
(6.2)	43	.56	.31	4.33	.01	
(6.3)	24	.55[f]	.30[f]	4.45	.05	

[a] To predict performance, variables in the situational, personal, and decision style classes in Table 3.4 were included as potential predictor variables in the stepwise regressions. In addition, variables U_{41} and U_{42} were included as potential predictors since these scales are classified as problem-solving in nature.

[b] Because of the wide range of values, standardized beta weights are presented rather than the actual regression coefficients. The beta weight represents the change in the dependent variable measured in number of standard deviations resulting from a standardized unit change in an independent variable with all other independent variables held constant.

[c] Numbers in parentheses are t statistics.

[d] Dummy (0, 1) variable; only the sign, not the magnitude, of the beta weight is meaningful.

[e] R^2 for the validation sample; originally the sample for Division A was divided into a 60% sample for analysis (n = 104) and a 40% sample for validation (n = 71). R_{t}^2 is the squared correlation of the actual values from the validation sample and the values predicted for the validation sample using the coefficients of regression Equation (6.1).

[f] Adjusted R, R^2.

findings do support the contention that decision style is associated with performance.

The results of predicting performance for the five indicators in the Branch Bank study are shown in Table 6.2.* Activism, exceeding limits, and the need for loan approvals for both managers and assistant managers, are positively associated with performance. These characteristics appear to describe a more aggressive and risk-taking individual; it is interesting to note that in the previous chapter the same variables were negatively associated with the use of information. Thus more aggressive members of management appear to use the information systems less and have higher performance than less aggressive members of management. Keeping personal records is also associated with performance in Equations 6.3 and 6.4 (Table 6.2), but the direction of the relationship is not consistent. However, the results support the contention of Proposition 12 that decision style is associated with performance.

PROPOSITION 13. PERSONAL AND SITUATIONAL VARIABLES

Background

In the preceding chapter we discussed Proposition 9 and saw that personal and situational factors are associated with differing levels of systems use and the likelihood of taking action. In this chapter we are interested in whether different personal and situational factors are associated with different levels of performance.

Evidence

Data on performance for sales representatives in the Sales Force study may be found in Table 6.1. In Division A higher performance is associated with sales representatives who have fewer accounts. Represen-

---

* The sample in this table consists of all branches for which both managers and assistant managers returned questionnaires. Because of problems with missing data on the questionnaire, the number of branches which could be included in this analysis is less than might be expected, given the number of responses for branch and assistant branch managers alone. Owing to missing data, some of the assistant manager responses could not be included in the regressions in Table 6.2; correlations among assistant manager actions and performance for these variables are shown in Table 6.3.

Table 6.2. Standardized Regression Predicting Performance from the Branch Bank Study[a]

(6.3) P_{52}^{bc} Adjusted percentage of commercial loan goal =	(6.4) P_{53} Adjusted percentage of installment loan goal =	(6.5) P_{54} Adjusted percentage of real estate loan goal =
−.31 I_{51} Age (2.14)[d]	−.18 I_{51} Age (1.87)	−.25 I_{52} Years at bank (2.85)
+.25 I'_{51} Age (2.53)	−.25 I'_{52} Years at bank (2.38)	−.19 I'_{53} Years in position (2.23)
+.34 I_{52} Years at bank (2.15)	−.14 I'_{55} Education (1.41)	+.19 D_{53} Activism (2.20)
−.28 I'_{52} Years at bank (1.60)	−.15 U'_{55} Enquiry system (1.68)	−.18 E_{53} Daily statement (call attention) (2.01)
−.49 I_{53} Years in position (.40)	−.19 D_{51}^{e} Keeps own records (2.07)	−.37 E_{54} Branch objectives (reallocate efforts) (3.09)
−.10 I_{54} Years at branch (.83)	+.16 D_{54} Makes exceptions (1.66)	+.44 E_{55} Monthly profit summary (reallocate efforts) (3.83)
−.32 I'_{55} Education (2.67)	+.18 E'_{53} Daily statement (call attention) (1.84)	+.15 V'_{53} Compensation based on goals (1.75)
+.17 D_{51}^{e} Keeps own records (1.79)	+.07 E_{56} Monthly deposit, loan balance, income/expense report (reallocate efforts) (.79)	
+.20 D_{53} Activism (2.13)		
+.12 U'_{55} Enquiry system (1.31)		
+.33 E_{52} Monthly deposit, loan balance, and income/expense report (call attention) (3.02)		
−.22 E_{53} Daily statement (call attention) (2.06)		
−.18 E'_{55} Monthly profit summary (reallocate efforts) (.18)		
+.17 V_{52} Involvement in setting goals (1.66)		
−.25 V'_{53} Compensation based on goals (2.42)		

(6.6)

P_{55} Adjusted percentage of demand deposit goal =

$-.18$	I_{51}	Age	(1.91)
$+.17$	I_{54}	Years at branch	(1.79)
$+.12$	U'_{55}	Enquiry system	(1.30)
$-.12$	U_{55}	Enquiry system	(1.28)
$+.20$	D_{55}	Needs approvals	(2.16)
$+.18$	E_{51}	Monthly profit summary (call attention)	(1.85)

(6.7)

P_{56} Adjusted percentage of savings goal =

$-.19$	P_{57}	Supervisor rating	(2.05)
$-.23$	I_{51}	Age	(2.45)
$+.18$	I_{54}	Years at branch	(1.88)
$+.17$	I_{55}	Education	(1.74)
$+.16$	E'_{54}	Branch objectives (reallocate efforts)	(1.69)
$+.13$	V_{52}	Involvement in setting goals	(1.33)

Equation	n	R	R^2	F	$p \leq$
6.3	107	.52	.27	2.26	.05
6.4	110	.43	.19	2.87	.05
6.5	110	.52	.27	5.41	.01
6.6	107	.37	.13	2.58	.05
6.7	111	.37	.14	2.83	.05

[a] To predict performance, variables in the personal, use (for the enquiry system only), decision style (D_{51}–D_{55}) action, and user perception classes in Table 3.5 were included as potential predictor variables in the stepwise regressions. (Situational variables had already been used to develop the adjusted performance data; see Chapter 3.)

[b] Because of the wide range of values, standardized beta weights are presented rather than the actual regression coefficients. The beta weight represents the change in the dependent variable measured in number of standard deviations resulting from a unit increase in an independent variable with all other independent variables held constant.

[c] Prime denotes assistant managers; all other variables are for managers.

[d] Numbers in parentheses are t statistics.

[e] Dummy (0, 1) variable; only the sign, not the magnitude, of the beta weight is meaningful.

Table 6.3. Assistant Manager Performance Pearson Correlations from the Branch Bank Study [a]

	P_{54} Adjusted Percentage of Real Estate Loan Goal	P_{55} Adjusted Percentage of Demand Deposit Goal	P_{56} Adjusted Percentage of Savings Goal
E_{52}' Monthly deposit, loan balance, income/expense report (call attention)	—	.16 (127)	—
E_{55}' Monthly profit summary (reallocate efforts)	.15 (133) [b]	.15 (133)	.17 (133)
E_{56}' Monthly deposit, loan balance, income/expense report (reallocate efforts)	—	.20 (127)	.16 (127)

[a] $P \leq .05$.
[b] Number of respondents is indicated in parentheses.

tatives with few accounts probably have better customers; and the sales representative can also concentrate more on his best accounts if his total number is smaller. Length of time in position is a consistent predictor of performance, either (1) sales representatives have some influence on performance and the data demonstrate learning or (2) more senior sales representatives are rewarded with better territories and accounts. In Division B, education appears to be positively associated with performance.

The data in Table 6.2 from the Branch Bank study also demonstrate an association between personal and situational factors and performance. High performance is negatively related to the age of managers and to assistant managers' length of service at the bank. Other variables like education and length of time at the branch are significantly associated with performance, but the direction of the association is not consistent. The data from both studies support the existence of a relationship between personal and situational factors and performance.

PROPOSITION 14. LOW PERFORMANCE

Background
In Chapter 2 we discussed problem-finding activities which frequently precede problem solving. A problem occurs when a difference

exists between the decisionmaker's normative model of what should exist and reality. One of the frequent uses of information systems is to high-light such differences, for example, a budget variance, poor performance this period compared with a comparable period in the past. Proposition 14 states that low performance should stimulate the use of information for problem finding.

Evidence

In the Sales Force study, variables U_{43} to U_{46} are classified as prob-lem-finding in nature and performance was included as a predictor of the use of this information in the regression analysis. In Table 5.2 perfor-mance is associated with usage in Equations 5.7, 5.10, 5.15, and 5.20. As predicted, the association is negative in each case; that is, low per-formers make greater use of this problem-finding information.

In the Branch Bank study virtually all the reports could be classified as problem-finding in nature. A weighted index of branch performance using the weights of the branch objectives system was included as a predictor of use in the regression equations in Table 5.3. This variable, P_{51}, is as-sociated with performance only in Equation 5.29, and the direction is negative as predicted.

The Laboratory Experiment provides longitudinal data to supplement the findings of the cross-sectional studies discussed above; the results of this study as shown in Table 6.4 provide a stronger argument for the causal implications of the proposition. Table 6.4 contains an analysis of the data displayed by the players in the second session of the graphic CRT treatments during the experiment. In this analysis the mean perfor-mance in each month before and after the data item was displayed is com-pared for the group displaying the data item and the group which did not choose to display the item. Significant results are shown in Table 6.4; a negative t value means that the group requesting a graph of the data item had lower performance than the group not viewing the graph and vice versa. For example, demand (G_{61}) in the first row of Table 6.4 was displayed by 26 out of 44 players in month 2. Profit for these 26 players viewing demand in month 2 was significantly lower in month 1 than for the group that did not display month 2 demand ($t = -1.91$). Profits for the group viewing demand in month 2 were also significantly lower in months 3 ($t = -2.31$) and 5 ($t = -2.35$) than were profits for the group not viewing month 2 demand. (Remember the sequence of events is to

Table 6.4. *t*-Statistics [a] for Profit for CRT Players Displaying Data versus Profit of Those Not Displaying Data

	Month				
	1	2	3	4	5
G_{61} Demand	P_{61} Profit −1.91 [c]	Display (n = 26) [b]	P_{63} Profit −2.31 [d] Display (n = 17) P_{63} Profit 2.31 [d]		P_{65} Profit −2.35 [d] P_{65} Profit −2.18 [d] Display (n = 17)
G_{62} Closing Inventory	P_{61} Profit −2.71 [e]	Display (n = 11) P_{62} Profit −1.83 [c]	Display (n = 13) P_{63} Profit 2.50 [d]		P_{65} Profit −1.89 [c]
G_{63} Sales	P_{61} Profit −2.00 [c]	P_{62} Profit −2.20 [d] P_{62} Profit −2.13 [d]	Display (n = 14)	Display (n = 12) Display (n = 15)	P_{65} Profit −1.80 [c]
G_{64} Industry Sales			Display (n = 18)	P_{64} Profit 3.29 [e] P_{64} Profit 2.14 [d]	P_{65} Profit 2.39 [d] Display (n = 13) P_{65} Profit 2.71 [e]
G_{65} GNP	P_{61} Profit −2.28 [d]		Display (n = 7) P_{63} Profit 2.87 [e] P_{63} Profit 3.31 [c]		Display (n = 2)
G_{66} GNP forecast		P_{62} Profit 2.30 [d]	Display (n = 9) P_{63} Profit 1.88 [c]		P_{65} Profit 1.91 [c]

	Month				
	1	2	3	4	5
	P_{61} Profit −2.36 [c]			Display (n = 6)	
G_{67} Production Index			Display (n = 21)	P_{64} Profit 1.88 [c]	
			P_{63} Profit 2.09 [d]		
	P_{61} Profit −1.77 [c]	P_{62} Profit −2.27 [c]		Display (n = 20)	
G_{68} Production index forecast		Display (n = 33)			P_{65} Profit −2.08 [d]
			Display (n = 28)		
			P_{63} Profit 2.21 [d]		
	P_{61} Profit −1.95 [c]			Display (n = 32)	P_{65} Profit −1.81 [c]
			P_{63} Profit 1.94 [c]		Display (n = 33)
G_{69} Substitute product index			Display (n = 11)	P_{64} Profit 2.24 [d]	
			P_{63} Profit 2.95 [c]		
			P_{63} Profit −1.75 [c]	Display (n = 10)	
All problem-solving information (G_{65}, G_{66}, G_{67}, G_{68})		Display (n = 9)			P_{65} Profit 2.21 [d]
			Display (n = 9)		
			P_{63} Profit −1.78 [c]		
				Display (n = 9)	P_{65} Profit 1.86 [c]

[a] A negative t value means that the group using the display had significantly lower profits than the group not using the display, while a positive t value means that the group viewing the graph had higher profits.

[b] n = number viewing display out of 44 players.

[c] $p \leq .10$.   [d] $p \leq .05$.   [e] $p \leq .01$.

display data at time t for the results of month $t - 1$; input is then prepared for time t based on these results.)

Demand, closing inventory, and sales can be graphed to show problems and to compare results for different periods. For example, what was the player's market share compared with his competition? What were this player's sales and what is his closing inventory? For these problem-finding graphs of demand (G_{61}), closing inventory (G_{62}), and sales (G_{63}), low performance is associated with the group displaying the data in 11 out of 13 instances in Table 6.4, though in only 5 of the instances did the significantly lower performance precede the display of the data item. It appears that problem-finding information is rather consistently associated with low performance. The results also suggest that, at least in the Laboratory Experiment, correcting a problem once it has been located is difficult; the display of problem-finding data was frequently associated with continued low performance after the data were viewed.

PROPOSITION 15. PROBLEM-SOLVING INFORMATION AND ACTION

Background
Proposition 15 states that the use of problem-solving information should be associated with performance if the user takes action consistent with the information. Problem-solving information helps a decisionmaker arrive at a solution after he has developed an understanding of the nature of the problem. To test Proposition 15 we need to identify problem-solving information and relate it to performance.

Evidence
If we refer again to Table 6.1, the results for sales representative performance show that problem-solving information (working with the customer in the store and performing a detailed analysis of the sales report by buying entity or an account) is not a significant predictor of performance in Division A or B. However, the use of the sales report to work with customers in the store is positively associated with performance in Division C. Division A is confronted with a very stable environment; one customer called the sales representatives in this division

"order takers," and division B is staffed primarily with sales representatives from Division A. Division C, however, faces the more volatile marketplace of women's fashions; sales representatives in Division C probably have greater influence on their performance than those in other divisions. Here the use of problem-solving information is positively associated with performance.

Earlier in the chapter we discussed the CRT monitor results for the Laboratory Experiment in Table 6.4; at that time we were interested primarily in problem-finding information. Most of the data items which could be graphed are problem-solving in nature (see the variables from G_{64} to the end of the table). In fact, the total of all the items graphed across all periods indicate that the three most frequently examined graphs were of problem-solving data.

In the problem-solving category, industry sales data can be used to help predict trends and demand. GNP and GNP forecast can provide the decisionmaker with an idea of how the simulated economy is progressing and what this means for his own company. The production index, production index forecast, and substitute product index all can be used by the player to forecast sales and solve the problems of how much product to ship and when to schedule arrivals.

In Table 6.4 seventeen out of twenty-six significant differences for problem-solving information are positive as predicted. Thirteen of the seventeen positive relationships (that is, greater profits for the group viewing the graph) occurred after the variable was displayed. Six of the nine negative relationships (that is, lower performance for the group viewing the graph) occurred before the display of the variable. These findings suggest that the use of problem-solving information may be stimulated by low performance and that the use of this information may contribute to improved performance. These results are only tentative, but the evidence suggests that further research is warranted.

The Branch Bank study provides data to test whether the likelihood of action taken on the basis of formal reports is associated with performance. Two types of action were considered: the likelihood of calling a problem to the attention of an employee, and the likelihood of reallocating branch efforts on the basis of information in reports. In each of the equations in Table 6.2, at least one variable indicating the likelihood of a branch manager or assistant branch manager taking action is significantly associated with performance. See also Table 6.3. Unfortunately, in such a cross-sectional study we cannot tell the significance of the direction of the association. There are some negative and some positive associations between the likelihood of taking action and performance. Was the likelihood of taking action stimulated by low performance? Was the action actually undertaken and has it not had a chance to correct the situation, or was the action not undertaken or inappropriate? Unfortunately, we shall have to await further longitudinal research to answer these questions, but it does appear that the likelihood of taking action based on an information system is associated with performance.

PROPOSITION 16. IRRELEVANT INFORMATION

Background

Several researchers have suggested that managers receive too much irrelevant information; they suffer from information overload (Ackoff, 1967). In Proposition 16 we suggest that irrelevant information can lead to low performance. A decisionmaker who spends time analyzing irrelevant information is using resources which could be better applied to the problem; time and energy are wasted and user frustration increases. It can be difficult to classify information that is irrelevant in advance, but one identifiable group in the Sales Force study appears to receive irrelevant data.

Evidence

Account executives in the Sales Force study generally have fewer than six accounts and often have only one or two clients. These accounts tend to be large and generate many orders because the customer is usually a department store chain or the equivalent. Interviews indicated that many account executives receive more timely, detailed, and pertinent data from their clients than from their employer. For example, the inventory control system in a department store may provide a report for the use of the account executive. Data from his own company's information system for the most part are not relevant to the account executive.

The regression results from predicting account executive performance in Divisions A and B are shown in Table 6.5 (only these divisions have a

Table 6.5. Standardized Regressions Predicting Account Executive Performance from the Sales Force Study [a]

Division A (6.8) P_{41}[b] Total Dollar Bookings 1972 Season=			Division B (6.9) P_{41} Total Dollar Bookings 1972 Season=		
−.37 S_{41}	Number of accounts	(2.55) [c]	−.26 S_{41}	Number of accounts	(1.88)
+.48 S_{42}	Number of buying entities	(3.75)	−.26 S_{43}	Time in territory	(1.51)
			+.20 S_{44}	Time in position	(1.21)
+.26 S_{44}	Time in position	(1.78)	−.28 U_{42}	Detailed analysis of buying entity/account	(1.50)
−.16 U_{41}	Working with customer in store	(1.24)	+.29 U_{43}	Overall progress	(1.63)
−.32 U_{44}	Summary this year vs. last	(2.31)	−.21 U_{44}	Summary this year vs. last	(1.31)
+.32 U_{46}	Cancellations	(2.29)	−.09 U_{45}	Planning	(.40)
			+.14 D_{42}[d]	Performs calculations on report	(.94)

Equation	n	R	R^2	F	$p \leq$
6.8	41	.68	.46	6.35	.001
6.9	22	.81[e]	.63[e]	6.76	.010

[a] To predict performance, variables in all of the classes in Table 3.4 were included as potential predictor variables in the stepwise regressions.
[b] Because of the wide range of values, standardized beta weights are presented rather than the actual regression coefficients. The beta weight represents the change in the dependent variable measured in standard deviations resulting from a standardized unit change in an independent variable with all other independent variables held constant.
[c] Numbers in parentheses are t statistics.
[d] Dummy (0, 1) variable; only the sign, not the magnitude, of the beta weight is meaningful.
[e] Adjusted R, R^2.

sufficient number of account executives for analysis.) Low levels of use for two and three usage variables in Equations 6.8 and 6.9 predict high performance in Divisions A and B, respectively. In Division A the use of cancellation information is positively associated with account executive performance; this finding is understandable as cancellations are instituted by the company as a result of undersupply, and the sales report is the only source of this information. In Division B the use of overall progress information is positively associated with performance; the account executive might have difficulty developing this information from the data provided by customers. Thus, even though we are dealing with only one study, the data offer some support for Proposition 16 and the predicted association between low levels of use of irrelevant data and high levels of performance.

SUMMARY

In this chapter we have been concerned with propositions relating to user performance; see Table 6.6. Proposition 12 on decision style and Proposition 13 on situational and personal variables and performance receive support from the data. The results for situational and personal fac-

Table 6.6. Summary of Propositions and Results for Chapter 6

Proposition	Support by Data [a,b]	Studies
12. Individuals with differing decision styles have differing levels of performance.	Reasonable support	Sales Force study
13. Different situational and personal factors lead to differing levels of performance.	Strong support	Sales Force study Branch Bank study
14. Low performance stimulates the use of problem-finding information produced by an information system.	Reasonable support	University study Branch Bank study Laboratory Experiment
15. The use of problem-solving information produced by an information system leads to high levels of performance if the user takes action consistent with the information.	Reasonable support	Sales Force study Branch Bank study Laboratory Experiment
16. For irrelevant information, low levels of use of an information system lead to high performance.	Some support	Sales Force study

[a] Scored as a continuum 1 2 3 4 5 6 7. (1. Rejected. 2. No evidence. 3. Weak support. 4. Some support. 5. Reasonable support. 6. Strong support. 7. Demonstrated beyond reasonable doubt.)

[b] In developing the rating, factors such as the number of studies, independence of data sources, interstudy consistency, research design, and strength of the findings were considered.

tors appear to be more consistent in direction for performance than for the use of information or the likelihood of taking action.

We also found support for Proposition 14 on the relationship between low levels of performance and the use of problem-finding data. In fact, there is some evidence from the Laboratory Experiment which suggests that low performance may provide a general stimulus to use information.

The data also support Proposition 15; the use of problem-solving information is associated with high performance. The likelihood of taking action is also significantly associated with performance. However, the research design in the Branch Bank study makes it difficult to answer interesting questions on the timing and effect of action and whether or not the action was actually taken.

Proposition 16 concerning irrelevant data was also supported. Data are available only for one subgroup within the Sales Force study, but this limited evidence does suggest that low levels of use of irrelevant data are associated with high performance.

The findings in this chapter support the classification of information into problem-finding and problem-solving categories. This distinction has important implications for systems design; the relevant information for the problem faced by the user must be provided if a system is to be successful.

SEVEN

implications for successful systems

THE DESCRIPTIVE MODEL

Research Findings

REVIEWING THE SUMMARY TABLES at the end of Chapters 4 through 6, we can see that the data from the six studies support the descriptive model of informations systems in the context of the organization. The evidence is consistent with each proposition in the model and provides support for the propositions. However, in several cases only one study furnished data on a proposition and, in some of the studies, only one data source was available. A number of the propositions, though, are supported by multiple studies, each using several independent sources of data which provide more substantial credibility for the results.

The most important findings of the preceding three chapters in terms of the key variables in the model are summarized in Table 7.1. The descriptive model of information systems in the context of the organization focuses on three classes of variables: user attitudes and perceptions, the use of systems, and user performance. The policies of the information services department and the technical quality of systems are associated with favorable user attitudes and perceptions. Favorable attitudes and perceptions and systems with high technical quality are associated with high levels of use of information systems. Finally, low performance is associated with high levels of use for problem-finding information while the

Table 7.1. Major Propositions Related to the Three Key Variable Classes in the Model

User attitudes and perceptions (Chapter 4)	
Proposition	*Support by data* [a]
2. ISD Policies	Reasonable support
5. Technical quality of systems	Strong support
Use of systems (Chapter 5)	
Proposition	*Support by data*
7. User attitudes and perceptions	Strong support
10. Technical quality of systems	Strong support
Performance (Chapter 6)	
Proposition	*Support by data*
14. Low performance—problem finding	Reasonable support
15. High use—problem solving	Reasonable support

[a] See Tables 4.5, 5.6, and 6.6 for details.

use of problem-solving information is positively associated with performance.

These major findings, along with the other results, indicate why so many information systems have failed. With the exception of variables associated with the technical quality of systems, all the variables we discussed have been organizational and behavioral in nature. Clearly, the results support the argument that technical problems have to be solved so that systems are of high technical quality. However, the model and results also argue that organizational behavior variables have to be considered if we are to design and operate successful systems. If we continue to ignore the majority or the variables in the model, it is likely that information systems will continue to fail.

Causal Implications

Unfortunately, we cannot claim to have tested the causal implications of the model with most of the results. In each instance we were careful to state that the data are consistent with the predictions of the model, not that a change in one variable caused movement in another variable. What can we say about causality from the results of the studies discussed in Chapters 4 through 6?

The University study included independent information services department ratings of systems quality, user perceptions of quality, and user attitudes. The evidence from this study supports the argument of a causal relationship between the quality of systems and user attitudes (Proposition 5). It is unlikely that user attitudes could lead directly to better systems quality as rated independently by the information services department staff. This independence of data sources is more supportive of a causal relationship than the associations between user perceptions and user attitudes measured by the single questionnaire administered to users in the other studies.

A priori reasoning also suggests that the personal and situational factors considered in Propositions 8 and 9 are responsible for different types of behavior. We can argue from a time perspective; the use of an information system could not cause personal factors like age and education though, over an extended period of time, use of an information system might change an individual's decision style. Situational factors are also likely to be causal variables when certain types of behavior are considered, at least in the short run. For example, working in a hub location might force a manager to take action based on formal information, though a third variable might influence being placed in a hub location and taking action. The manager might have been chosen for this position because he has a demonstrated history of taking effective action in other locations.

Finally, the Laboratory Experiment provides some longitudinal evidence of causality when the sequence of graphical displays and the associated performance differences are examined. The experiment presents stronger support for the argument that low performance stimulates the use of information than do the cross-sectional studies. However, the results are not overwhelming, as only a few of the possible relationships between performance and the display of data items were significant. The results, though, are generally in the predicted direction.

While the data offer some support for several of the causal implications in the model, the results so far must be considered tentative. Further research is needed to explore each of the propositions in greater depth, particularly longitudinal field studies and further laboratory experiments.

The Contribution of Information Systems

In several earlier chapters we stressed the importance of information systems. On the basis of the evidence from the studies, do information systems really make a contribution to the decisionmaker and the organization? Relationships between the use of information systems and performance were found in all three of the studies which included performance variables. However, the relationships were not strong in the field studies; many independent variables other than the use of an information system are associated with performance. The evidence is more favorable under the controlled environment of the Laboratory Experiment. However, we can still ask whether the large investment of resources in information systems made by organizations is justified.

There are several reasons why investments in information systems may be worthwhile. First, the data on associations between use of a system and performance in the field studies are from a sample of users all of whom receive information. Only in the laboratory game did some decisionmakers choose to use information while others did not. In the field studies all the subjects received the reports, and we have no data to determine whether there is a significant difference in performance between a group which receives reports and a group which does not. To answer this question in a field study we need a comparison group of similar users facing a comparable environment who do not receive output from an information system. From a research design standpoint, such a situation is extremely difficult to find.

We also studied the complex relationship between performance and the use of information systems. For example, we found different relationships between performance and problem-finding and problem-solving information. Are there other roles for information not reflected in the data discussed so far?

In one of the first sets of laboratory experiments, two MBA groups played the Transportation Game. In period 2, one group received no additional information and the other received added reports. For both of the treatment groups, period 2 play began at the same starting point as period 1, though the reports for the first playing period were not available. The groups exhibited no significant difference in mean profits, but the group that received additional reports had a significantly lower variance in profits.*

We suspect that the group which received no additional reports had a greater variance in profits because some of the more capable players

* In later experiments, period 2 play was started at a new point in the game rather than as a replay of the first period.

remembered salient data from the first round. Others did not capitalize on the experience of the first playing period and fell behind in profits. The group receiving the added information had a lower variance because everyone had new information available; less individual effort was required to obtain information since it was provided on the added reports. It is also possible that the information on the reports channeled the thinking of the players receiving the added reports, reducing the variance in performance. Variance can be thought of as risk or uncertainty; since decisionmakers and organizations try to reduce uncertainty, we can speculate that information systems might well contribute to reducing risk by lowering performance variances.

Information can also serve to comfort a decisionmaker and signal that performance is within acceptable ranges. To the extent that such an observation leads to complacency, it is detrimental to performance. However, if receiving confirmation builds confidence and increases expectations of goal achievement, then motivation and performance should increase.

Additional evidence of the importance of information systems to decisionmakers and the organization is found in the heavy use of systems in the studies. Questionnaire scales for the use of information ranged from 1 to 7, and the intercepts of the regression equations predicting use were high. In the University study, for example, the intercepts for predicting use of the batch systems were 4.80 and 1.07. Responses to the open-ended comments on the questionnaries also testified to the importance of the systems under study. Several sales representatives in the Sales Force study who had recently joined the company mentioned that they now received much better information; their old employers provided almost no information on clients or performance.

There are multiple roles for information systems in an organization; in fact, we even found multiple roles for information for the same group of users. For example, some sales representatives kept item level records to supplement the sales information system in the Sales Force study. Given the variety of uses of information and the importance of information to decisionmaking, it seems safe to conclude that information systems are important to the organization. Clearly, though, each individual system has to be justified before development. The attractiveness of a proposed information system depends on a number of variables, many of which are unique to the organization and the decisionmakers involved.

USE OF THE MODEL

System Failures

The descriptive model of Chapter 2 has received substantial support from the six studies discussed in this book, with the reservations expressed earlier in this chapter on causality. If we accept the validity of the model on the basis of this evidence, what are the implications?

Chapter 2 presented a brief scenario of how information systems might fail in an organization; the model and data suggest some important reasons why information systems do frequently fail. First, multiple parties, including management, users, and the information services department staff, are involved in the design and operation of information systems. All of these groups must work together to develop and operate successful systems.

Second, a number of variables are involved in the design and operation of successful systems. The complex relationships among technical, behavioral, situational, and personal factors all must be considered. If any variable is ignored, systems are likely to fail.

In the next two sections of this chapter we consider some of the implications of the model for operations and systems design activities. Many of the implications are supported directly by the data, while others are deduced from the relationships proposed by the model. All the implications are based on the importance of favorable user attitudes and perceptions, high levels of system use, and performance. (These points represent some of the possible implications of the model; there are undoubtedly other guidelines for action which can be derived from the model.) Our goal is to develop successful information systems which have a high level of use and make a positive contribution to decisionmakers and the organization.

Operations

The operation of existing information systems is an important activity. The information services department provides a service, and users form attitudes from their contact with operations; it should be easy and enjoyable for the user to use systems. The model and data suggest the following guidelines for operations (they are based primarily on the importance of service quality).

1. Require the information services department to publish and adhere to a service schedule for each application. For batch systems, each user should be guaranteed a time when output will be returned if the user meets input schedules. On-line systems should be available as scheduled.

2. Operate reliable systems; if there are continued problems in running an application, fix the problem or consider reprogramming the application. For on-line systems, provide backup if downtime is a problem; users become very dependent on fast response systems and are intolerant of failures.

3. Develop user representatives for applications to interface the user with the information services department. For any given system, no matter what the problem, the user should be able to contact a single representative of the information services department who is responsible for seeing that the problem is solved.

4. Plan for changes to existing systems as users gain experience with them, and allocate a portion of the budget for changes. Try to originate changes; for example, monitor user reactions to determine what modifications are needed.

5. Consider the use of a steering committee to set priorities for the operation of systems.

6. Provide sufficient computer capacity to meet special requests and peak processing loads. The ability to respond quickly to special jobs is one highly visible sign of responsiveness and high quality service.

7. Be certain that existing systems are operating at a satisfactory level of performance as evaluated by users before beginning the development of new systems.

Systems Design

Systems design is crucial to the organization and to the development of successful information systems. The control and processing of information is vitally important to the organization's success and survival. The systems design process is a creative activity which involves a number of individuals from different areas in the organization. Several important design considerations based on the model and the results of the studies should be stressed.

1. Let the user be the source of systems wherever possible; if the user initiates a system he will have more commitment to design, implementation, and use.

2. Consider the use of a steering committee of users and the information services department staff to allocate resources and make decisions on proposed applications.

3. Let the user design the system if possible. The information services staff should act as a catalyst and map the user's functional and logical design into manual procedures and computer programs (Lucas, 1974c).

4. In designing systems, delineate and study decisions and user actions, not only the flow of information and documents.

5. Consider and diagnose the multiple roles of information for different decisionmakers and decisionmaking situations. For example, we have distinguished between problem-finding and problem-solving information. Exception reporting might be appropriate for problem-finding data. For problem-solving information, users might respond favorably if able to obtain data as needed, possibly through batch retrieval packages or an on-line enquiry facility.

6. Be selective in developing output requirements; do not overload users; that is, be sensitive to the relevance of information and try to avoid sending irrelevant data to decisionmakers.

7. Design flexible systems; the evidence suggests that there are different needs and requirements for different individuals in the organization. An attempt should be made to provide options for users, for example, through special retrieval programs. Plan systems with disaggregated data bases and let the user select the output format and the level of summarization he desires.

8. Consider different personal and situational factors and decision styles in developing systems. Provide enough flexibility that users in different environments and with different levels of experience, education, etc., can benefit from the system. Consider personal and situational factors in planning the implementation of the system; for example, see Mumford and Ward (1968).

9. Stress the development of favorable user attitudes during the design phase and adopt user criteria for measuring the success of the system. Plan carefully for implementation and consider the impact of the system in advance.*

10. Develop a good user interface; for example, consider the use of

* For a further discussion of the adoption of user criteria for evaluating a system and the approach of having users design a system, see Lucas (1974c).

on-line systems to reduce the burden of input and output on users. Make it easy mechanically to use the system.

11. Include training in the design of the system, possibly by having the user design team train others so that high levels of use of a system will be possible.

12. After implementation, be sure the system operates according to specifications. Work with the operations staff to monitor user reactions and make necessary changes to the system.

Intervention

The guidelines above have been suggested to improve the operation and design of information systems. However, these steps are not sufficient to prevent information systems from failing. The spirit of the recommendations is of major importance; a set of attitudes and an approach to information systems activities which consciously considers the context of the organization underlie the recommendations. The three major groups in the organization concerned with information systems (management, users, and the information services department staff) must adopt this perspective and cooperate to see that recommendations like those above are followed.

What can these three groups do to prevent the failure of information systems? Where should we intervene and how do we create an environment conducive to the implementation of the recommendations? It is hard to modify user attitudes directly since they are developed in response to interactions and experience. While minimal use of a system can be required, the best results come from self-motivated voluntary use. Though the causal arguments of the model have not been demonstrated beyond doubt, from a practical standpoint we can suggest some appropriate actions for each of the three groups in the organization who must cooperate to prevent the failure of information systems.

Management has the responsibility to set goals and priorities for the information services department and users. What types of systems should be stressed, and are the systems under development consistent with the overall goals and objectives of the organization? Management also has the responsibility to influence users and the information services department by participating in decisions about information systems, including decisions on the selection of new applications and on systems design issues. Management should also provide the needed resources, especially manpower, so that users can participate in systems design activities. Finally, management influences users and the information services department. Users should be rewarded for their cooperation and participation in design. The information services department staff should be rewarded for the design of successful, user-oriented systems, not just for implementing a system.

Users have the responsibility to learn about information systems, contribute to their operation and development, and participate in making intelligent decisions about them. Users need to participate in systems design and, wherever possible, should design systems themselves. User input is necessary to develop a high quality system; participation in design makes implementation easier and stimulates greater use of the system. To encourage use of systems, users could form groups for different systems; the groups meet and trade ideas on how best to use the output of the system. Sales representatives could hold meetings to see how other representatives use a sales report to work with customers, plan calls, allocate sales efforts, organize territories, etc. For the user, it is more meaningful to hear another user describe how a system is used than to read it in a training manual!

The information systems department has much of the responsibility for designing and operating successful information systems. The recommendations made in the two preceding sections of this chapter are basically aimed at the information services department. The emphasis of the development should be on the quality of service as perceived by users. The individual differences among users in situational, personal, and decision style variables should be understood and accepted by the staff. The various roles of information and the importance of favorable user attitudes should also be stressed.

For the information services department the basis of our recommended approach is a philosophy of user-oriented design and operations. Quality rather than quantity is emphasized. If this approach is followed, systems will probably take longer to develop and will cost more. However, if the model is correct, such information systems should be more heavily used and should make a greater contribution to the decisionmaker and the organization than do existing systems.

SYSTEMS DESIGN AND RESEARCH

The systems design activity is really a research and development effort. An attempt is made to determine user needs and requirements; then an abstract model of a process is created in the form of computer programs and manual procedures. The tools and techniques used in the six studies to conduct research on systems design can be used actively in systems design, itself (Lucas, 1971; Lucas and Plimpton, 1972).

The information services department might administer tests to a sample of decisionmakers to assess their decision style before beginning the design of a system. A survey would contribute to the selection of the members of a design team ensuring that a variety of views are represented. The results would also contribute to predictions of how various potential users in the organization might react to the development and implementation of a new system (Mumford and Ward, 1968). Finally, the results could assist in planning options and in determining what type of flexibility needs to be included in the system.

The design team could also make use of survey techniques to develop specifications for a system. The types of information used by decisionmakers could be determined through a series of interviews. The results from the interviews would then be used to develop a survey instrument which is administered to all potential users to define decisions, present sources of information and the action to be taken on the basis of the data. Performance measures could also be developed, either objective measures like sales or profits, or subjective indicators such as supervisor or peer ratings. Data from the survey would be correlated with the performance rating in order to determine what types of information and what actions are associated with performance. Here we are interested in problem-finding, problem-solving, and irrelevant information. Certainly, information associated with high levels of performance should receive careful attention and high priority in the development of an information system.

There are a variety of ways to collect data for constructing specifications for an information system. The results of devoting extensive efforts to such research activities should be less redesign, more relevant information from systems, and greater levels of system use.

CONCLUSIONS

We have developed a descriptive model of information systems in the context of the organization and have tested the model with data from six studies. The data from these studies are highly consistent with the predictions of the model. The results help us to understand the reasons why so many information systems have failed: we have concentrated too much on technology and have ignored crucial organizational behavior problems.

The model and findings stress the fact that information systems exist within the context of an organization. To design and operate successful information systems, three major groups in the organization must cooperate: management, users, and the information services department need to consider the organizational and technical variables we have discussed. Information systems have a tremendous potential for users and for the organization. Our challenge is to understand why information systems fail so that we can develop and operate successful systems.

APPENDIX

statistical analysis

INTRODUCTION

WE PRESENT A BRIEF OVERVIEW of the statistical techniques used for data analysis in Chapters 4 through 6. For a more complete discussion of these topics the reader is referred to any good text on statistical analysis, such as Blalock (1960).

Statistical Significance

All the studies discussed in the book make use of sampling theory in some way; that is, rather than administer a questionnaire to all branch bank managers, a sample was drawn. Sampling makes it possible to conduct research on a much more economical basis. Tests of statistical significance can be used as a guide to the generalization of the sample results to the entire population.

Frequently, researchers are not too precise in defining their target population. For example, we have allowed the reader to judge whether the results from a sample of bank managers can only be generalized to other bank managers in the bank studied, or whether conditions are similar enough across organizations that the population can be defined as all bank managers or even managers in general.

When inferring from a sample, we generally have in mind a null hypothesis which we are trying to reject. To be conservative, stringent requirements are placed on rejecting this null hypothesis. As an example

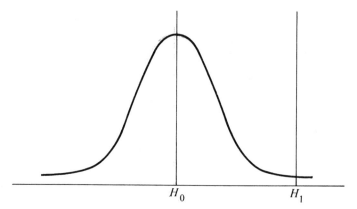

Figure A.1. Hypothesis testing.

of such a hypothesis, consider the statement that there is no association between A and B. The objective of the statistical test is to reject the null hypothesis of no association and accept an alternative hypothesis that there is an association. For all the statistical tests in the monograph, we are attempting to reject this type of null hypothesis; that is, there is no difference in means, no correlation, etc.

Because we are drawing a sample, there is a probability of an error. In Figure A.1, let H_0 be the null hypothesis that there is no difference between the mean of some hypothesized distribution and the mean of a sample distribution of interest. Suppose we draw a random sample and compute the mean H_1. There are two types of errors that we can make. In a Type I error we can reject the null hypothesis, given that the null hypothesis is true. That is, H_1 occurred because of our sampling procedure, not because there is a difference between the mean in the null hypothesis and the observed sample mean.

A Type II error occurs when we accept the null hypothesis, given that it is false. That is, we are unwilling to reject the null hypothesis because, owing to chance, the observed mean was not convincing enough for rejection even though there is a difference between H_1 and the null hypothesis, H_0.

For testing a hypothesis we refer to the probability of a Type I error as α and the probability of a Type II error as β. Most frequently a value of

α is established for the test; it is much more difficult to assign a value to β. Because of conservatism we usually report α, that is, the probability that we falsely reject the null hypothesis and accept the alternative hypothesis. It is common in research of this type to use an α of .05 or lower, but occasionally for small samples we include an α of .10. An α of .05 means that, 5% of the time, we shall reject the null hypothesis incorrectly; that is, we say there is an association when none exists.

We should point out that statistical significance refers only to sampling; there are many other sources of errors which are not reflected in α, such as our inability to draw a completely random sample, errors in measurement, and violations of the assumptions underlying statistical tests. The reader should also be aware that statistical significance says very little about practical significance. In extremely large samples a very small difference may turn out to be statistically significant. The question the reader must ask is whether or not such a small difference has any practical significance for drawing conclusions.

Mean and Variance

Two basic statistics are important in all the statistical tests we shall discuss. The mean measures the central tendency of a statistical distribution and is identical with the familiar arithmetic average. For a series of observations $x_1, x_2, \ldots, x_n$ the mean, x, is defined by

$$\bar{x} = \frac{\sum\limits_{i=1}^{n} x_i}{n}$$

The variance is a measure of dispersion about the mean; in Figure A.2 both distributions have the same mean, but the unshaded curve has a much higher variance. Mathematically, the variance s^2 is defined as

$$s^2 = \frac{\sum\limits_{i=1}^{n} (x_i - \bar{x})^2}{n}$$

The familiar standard deviation is the square root of the variance.

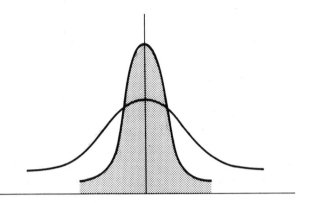

Figure A.2. Identical means, different variances.

STATISTICAL TECHNIQUES

In the book we use three major types of statistics to describe (1) difference in means (*t* tests), (2) associations among two variables (correlation), and (3) associations among one dependent and several independent variables (multiple regression). Each of these statistical techniques is discussed briefly below.

Difference in Means

For several of the propositions stated we are interested in whether or not two means differ; for example, do mean attitudes and perceptions of users of on-line systems differ from attitudes and perceptions of non-users? Consider the hypothetical distributions for the perceptions of input quality on the part of users and nonusers of on-line systems as shown in Figure A.3.

We would feel more confident saying that a difference exists in the means in Figure A.3a than in Figure A.3b, where the distributions have significant overlap. In rejecting the null hypothesis and stating that a difference exists, we need to consider both the mean and the variance of the two distributions. A number called the *t* statistic can be computed which allows us to test for the statistical significance of an observed difference in means.

In addition to this example of testing the difference in the means of two groups, we might also want to test to see if a coefficient in a regression

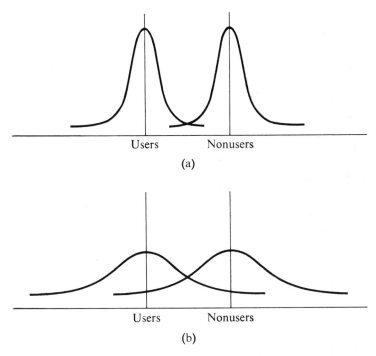

Figure A.3. Similar mean differences, different variances.

equation is significantly different from zero. The *t* test is also used for this purpose.

Correlation

In many instances we are interested in the existence and strength of the association between two variables; for example, are favorable user attitudes associated with the use of information systems? A statistic known as the Pearson correlation coefficient (r) is one measure of association. This coefficient ranges from -1 to $+1$ in value and is independent of measurement units. A -1 correlation signifies a perfect inverse relationship, a 0 correlation means there is no association, and a $+1$ correlation indicates a perfect positive relationship. Figure A.4 shows examples of several possible correlations. The square of the correlation coefficient represents the percentage of the variance in the dependent variable explained by the independent variable.

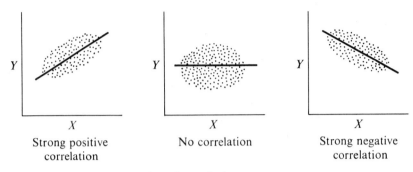

| Strong positive correlation | No correlation | Strong negative correlation |

Figure A.4. Examples of correlation.

Regression

In the regression analysis in the text we are trying to find a linear relationship between a series of independent variables and a single dependent variable. For illustrative purposes, consider the two-variable case with an equation of the form $y = a + bx$. Suppose we have collected the data shown in Figure A.5. We could fit a line which would have the desired equation through the points as shown. While more than one approach could be used to fit the line, in regression analysis we minimize the squared deviation of the observations from the line in the vertical direction. The dashed line shows this deviation for one of the data points in Figure A.5.

In multiple regression analysis we generalize the two-variable case to one in which there are multiple independent variables; our equation has the form

$$y = a + b_1 x_1 + b_2 x_2 + \cdots + b_n x_n$$

One advantage of this analysis is that the contribution of each independent variable is estimated in combination with those of other independent variables. The simple zero-order correlation coefficient discussed above considers only two variables at a time. Because many of the propositions in the model concern relationships among several variables, regression techniques are used for much of the data analysis in the book.

Variables in the regression equation may have widely differing units of measure, for example, a sales representative's dollar bookings for the year versus his response from 1 to 7 on a questionnaire; the resulting co-

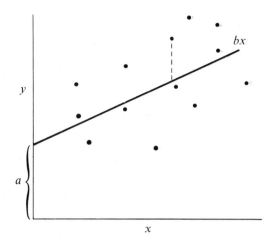

Figure A.5 Regression example $y = a + bx$.

efficients of the equation can be hard to interpret. To avoid this problem, many of our regression results are presented in standardized form without the intercept term a and with each coefficient b replaced by its standardized beta weight. The beta weight indicates how much change in a dependent variable measured in number of its standard deviation units would be produced by a change of one standard deviation unit in an independent variable controlling for all other independent variables.

In the analysis in the text we have used a stepwise regression algorithm. The dependent variable and a set of potential independent variables are first defined. The stepwise regression procedure then selects independent variables one at a time which provide the best possible prediction of the dependent variable. The multiple regression algorithm was terminated when the coefficient of an incoming variable would no longer be significant at the .10 level based on a one-tailed t test. In some of the equations there are insignificant variables due to changes when new variables entered; however, all coefficients were significant on first entering the equation. (The signs of the variables remained the same in almost all cases, even though the significance level changed.)

Several statistical tests are associated with regression analysis. An F statistic based on variances is used to determine the statistical significance of the final regression equation as a whole. A t statistic can be used to test each individual coefficient to see if it is significantly different from zero. Finally, R measures the goodness of fit of the equation to the data; the squared goodness of fit statistic (R^2) can be thought of as the percentage of the variation in the dependent variable explained by all the independent variables together. When the sample size is very small, R^2 is inflated; for small samples we present an adjusted R^2 which eliminates this bias.

references*

Ackoff, R. L. 1967. "Management Misinformation Systems." *Management Science*, 14 (4): B147–56.

Anthony, R. 1965. *Planning and Control Systems: A Framework for Analysis.* Boston: Division of Research, Graduate School of Business Administration, Harvard University.

Ashenhurst, R. (ed.) 1972. "Curriculum Recommendations for Graduate Professional Programs in Information Systems." *Comm. ACM*, 15 (5): 363–98.

Blalock, H. 1960. *Social Statistics.* New York: McGraw-Hill Book Co.

Brady, R. 1967. "Computers in Top-Level Decision Making." *Harvard Business Review*, (July–Aug.): 67–76.

Churchill, N. C., J. H. Kempster, and M. Uretsky. 1969. *Computer-Based Information Systems for Management: A Survey.* New York: National Association of Accountants.

Dearden, J., W. McFarlan, and W. Zani. 1971. *Managing Computer-Based Information Systems.* Homewood, Ill.: Richard D. Irwin.

Dickson, G., and R. Powers. 1973. "MIS Project Management: Myths, Opinions, and Reality." In W. McFarlan, R. Nolan, and D. Norton, *Information Systems Administration.* New York: Holt, Rinehart and Winston.

Doktor, R., and W. F. Hamilton. 1973. "Cognitive Style and the Acceptance of Management Science Recommendations." *Management Science*, 19 (8): 884–94.

Hardin, E. 1960. "The Reaction of Employees to Office Automation." *Monthly Labor Review*, 83: 925–32.

Hickson, P. J., C. R. Hennings, C. A. Lee, R. E. Schneck, and J. M. Pennings. 1971. "A Strategic Contingencies Theory of Interorganizational Power." *Administrative Science Quarterly*, 16 (2): 216–29.

* Only references specifically cited in the text are included here; for a more complete bibliography, the reader is referred to Lucas (1974c).

Jones, M. M., and E. R. McLean. 1970. "Management Problems in Large-Scale Software Development Projects." *Sloan Management Review*, 11 (3): 1–16.

Kay, R. H. 1969. "The Management and Organization of Large Scale Software Development Projects." *AFIPS Conf. Proc.* (SJCC), 34: 425–33. Montvale, N.J.; AFIPS Press.

Lawler, E. E., and R. J. Hackman. 1969. "Impact of Employee Participation in the Development of Pay Incentive Plans: A Field Experiment." *J. Applied Psychology*, 53 (6): 467–71.

Leavitt, H. J., and T. L. Whisler. 1958. "Management in the 1980's." *Harvard Business Review*, (Nov.–Dec.): 41–48.

Lucas, H. C., Jr. 1971. "A User Oriented Approach to Systems Design." *Proc. 1971. ACM Nat. Conf.*, 325–38.

———. 1973a. *Computer Based Information Systems in Organizations*. Palo Alto: Science Research Associates.

———. 1973b. "The Problems and Politics of Change: Power, Conflict and the Information Services Subunit." In F. Gruenberger (ed.), *Effective versus Efficient Computing*. Englewood Cliffs, N. J.: Prentice-Hall.

———. 1973c. "User Reactions and the Management of Information Services." *Management Informatics*, 2 (Aug.): 165–72.

———. 1974a. "An Empirical Study of an Information Systems Framework." *Decision Sciences*, 5 (1): 102–14.

———. 1974b. "User Reactions to Computer Operations." *Sloan Management Review*, 15 (3): 59–67.

———. 1974c. *Toward Creative Systems Design*. New York: Columbia University Press.

———. 1974d. "Systems Quality, User Reactions and the Use of Information Systems." *Management Informatics*, 3 (4): 207–12.

———. 1975a. "Performance and the Use of an Information System." *Management Science* (in press).

———, and R. B. Plimpton. 1972. "Technological Consulting in a Grass Roots, Action Oriented Organization." *Sloan Management Review*, 14 (1): 17–36.

Mann, F. C., and L. K. Williams. 1960. "Observations on the Dynamics of a Change to Electronic Data Processing Equipment." *Administrative Science Quarterly*, 5 (2): 217–56.

Mason, R. D., and I. I. Mitroff. 1973. "A Program for Research on Management Information Systems." *Management Science*, 19 (5): 475–87.

Mumford, E., and O. Banks. 1967. *The Computer and the Clerk*. London: Routledge & Kegan Paul.

———, and T. B. Ward. 1968. *Computers: Planning for People*. London: B. T. Batsford.

Pounds, W. F. 1969. "The Process of Problem Finding." *Industrial Management Review*, 11 (1): 1–20.

Scheflen, K. C., E. E. Lawler, and R. J. Hackman. 1971. "Long Term Impact of Employee Participation in the Development of Pay Incentive Plans: A Field Experiment Revisited." *J. Applied Psychology*, 55 (3): 182–86.

Scott Morton, M. S. 1971. *Management Decision Systems*. Boston: Division of Research, Graduate School of Business Administration, Harvard University.

Simon, H. 1965. *The Shape of Automation for Men and Management*. New York: Harper and Row.

Trist, E. L. 1963. *Organizational Choice*. London: Tavistock Publications.

Walton, R. E., and J. P. Dutton. 1969. "The Management of Interdepartmental Conflict: A Model and Review." *Administrative Science Quarterly*, 14 (1): 73–84.

Whisler, T. L., and H. Meyer. 1967. *The Impact of EDP on Life Company Organization*. New York: Life Office Management Association.

index